Amazing Grays Speak Out

When I read Maggie's book, it was as though she had read my mind, brought up all the concerns and dilemmas I was facing. I immediately felt like I had company on this confusing journey. There were real answers here…well-researched explanations of my options, expressed so clearly from a real grown woman's perspective that it was as though I had taken the years to study them myself…only better.

Susan Magee, *voice teacher*

Reading *Amazing Grays* is like sharing a glass of wine with a girlfriend, and laughing your way through a heart-to-heart talk about what really matters as we age. With humor, tenderness, and great vulnerability on her part, Maggie encourages us to challenge our old ways of seeing things—so we can truly embrace the next 50 years and live them with gusto!

Colleen Campbell, *quantum biofeedback specialist*

As a business owner and seminar leader, I highly recommend all women over 40 read Maggie Crane's book *Amazing Grays*! Understanding who we are and who we are becoming is imperative to living in joy and embracing all the changes we experience as we traverse our life path. The tips and useful tools found in this book can make the difference between tentatively creeping forward and striding into the future with great confidence and a sense of security.

Rebecca Drake, *president of Bank Leadership Training*

Maggie Rose Crane humorously empowers women to look beyond their mirrors and to enjoy the personal challenges of maturing responsibly. *Amazing Grays* is to be kept by the side of every boomer's bed—to read and reread—while you lovingly and laughingly journey along!

Sharon Feingold, *retired elementary teacher*

Maggie Crane's book *Amazing Grays* is a road map for finding your own peace, adjusting your attitude and taking the journey like a class act. We can rail against pesky gravity, passing time and life's disappointments but in the end its all about accepting change, creating balance and finding value. Maggie's book will help you sort through fact and fiction to come up with a real life approach so that as you live longer you'll feel better doing it!

Mary Jo Korn, *aging physical therapist*

Maggie Crane has opened up her heart and allowed us to share in her journey with breathtaking honesty. Choosing to embrace the fresh perspectives in her book will allow you to be more courageous in the face of change, and embrace the authentic you. With her elegantly straightforward style of writing, Maggie helps take us to a place of real joy…a step beyond happiness. As I continue to surrender outdated parts of myself on my own journey through aging, I am reminded by this book that this season in life can truly give us back to ourselves.

Sharon Kearin, *professional dancer and movement educator*

If you are wrestling with the issue of no longer coloring your hair, you will be richly rewarded with the research that Maggie Crane has done and the way she weaves humor into the facts. You will be delightfully surprised at the way she encourages you to delve into issues much deeper than the color of your hair. My guess is that you will return to these pages again and again for the wisdom they impart and the fresh perspective they offer.

Elaine Bonoma, *financial planner*

Having watched my older sister (Maggie) grow out her silver hair—I was inspired to do the same. Reading her book has helped me understand that my hair color is not what makes me—*me*. I love my silver hair! By sharing her perspectives on aging well—Maggie has given me a roadmap to follow. As a result, I'm having the time of my life!

Carla Vine, *retired kindergarten paraprofessional*

As I was proofreading Maggie's book, I realized that she was speaking to me. I'd been questioning my career choice for the past year, and her comments on joy and authenticity and living from the heart really hit home. After taking a good look at what really makes me happy, I realized it was time to change course and create opportunities to do more of what I love. So now I spend less time scowling at my computer and more time playing at the dog park!

Carolyn Fox, *proofreader and pet sitter*

AMAZING GRAYS

A **Woman's** Guide to Making the Next 50 THE BEST 50*

* Regardless of your hair color!

MAGGIE ROSE CRANE

FTA
PRESS

SAN DIEGO, CALIFORNIA

S

This book contains general information and is not intended to be, nor should be, used as a substitute for specific medical advice. It is recommended that you consult a health-care professional before undertaking any medical protocol or exercise program.

Library of Congress Control Number: 2007931310
ISBN 978-0-9660874-99

Edited by Adriane Smith, adrianesmith@cox.net
Cover and interior design by Troy Scott Parker, CimarronDesign.com

Published by FTA Press, a division of CBGI
San Diego, California, USA
858-487-9017
858-592-0689 Fax
For bulk book orders, please email: orderbooks@FTAPress.com

Printed in the United States of America
Printing last digit: 10 9 8 7 6 5 4 3 2 1

This book includes information from the following sources:

Excerpts from *The Wisdom of Menopause* by Christiane Northrup, M.D., copyright © 2001, 2006 by Christiane Northrup. Used by permission of Bantam Books, a division of Random House, Inc.

Excerpts from *The Sexy Years* by Suzanne Somers, copyright © 2004 by Suzanne Somers. Used by permission of Crown Publishers, a division of Random House, Inc.

Counsel on hormone and supplement information provided by Dr. Neil Hirschenbein of the LaJolla Institute of Comprehensive Medicine, www.LJI.md, 858-546-8055.

⚜

*This book is dedicated to the generations
of women who will follow in our
collective footsteps,
and to the women of my family who
follow my own.
May our generation stand as a shining
example of joyful, authentic and
mindful living—at any age!*

*To my daughter Claire and my
granddaughters, Lyla and Macy,
may you age with grace,
knowing that your true beauty
lies in your character and your deeds.
Live life with gusto!*

Contents

Acknowledgments

I F I'VE LEARNED ONE thing in the process of writing this book, it's that life becomes even more amazing when shared with kindred spirits.

Lerissa Patrick took my fragile first beginnings of this book and helped me mold them into something meaningful. Through her thoughtful coaching and skillful editing, I was able to craft a good start. Her willingness to serve as a sounding board throughout this process has been invaluable, and helped me become a better writer.

My editor, Adriane Smith, is wise way beyond her 30 years. Her knowledge, spiritual grounding and incredible editing skills have allowed me to say things more gracefully and succinctly than I ever could have without her. She stuck with me through many a rough patch, and during it all maintained her centeredness. Saying thank you hardly seems enough.

Carolyn Fox did a wonderful job copy editing and proofing the final manuscript, and her suggestions brought more clarity to the message.

To the wonderful women who read my early manuscripts and offered both encouragement and feedback, I bow in gratitude. Each of you has helped make this book what it is today, and you have a special place in my heart for your willingness to give me your honest opinions. Thanks to:

Elaine Bonoma, Stephanie Cline, Rebecca Drake, Sharon Feingold, Billie Frances, Sharon Kearin, MaryJo Korn, Alanna Lal, Linnea Long, Susan Magee, and Carla Vine.

I'm grateful to Chad Thompson for the photographs he took that capture the authentic me, wrinkles, crinkles, silver hair and all, in a way that honors the woman I've become.

We have Troy Scott Parker to thank for his beautiful cover and interior design of this book. With his considerable sense of style and artistic flair, he helped to put a distinctive face on my work.

Many thanks to my hairstylist, Pam Benson, who totally supported my decision to go gray. I needed that!

I am grateful to my blended family. The lessons were tough, and not always pretty, but they helped me to grow. It brings me joy to see how each of you turned out to be really good people with incredible talents. I offer kudos to Andy and his beautiful wife Julia, to Jason and his main squeeze Camille, to Claire and her wonderful husband Bromi, and to the gifts that keep on giving—my granddaughters Lyla and Macy.

To my husband, Tom, I owe a debt of gratitude. He gave me encouragement, love, feedback, food (when I got so engrossed in my writing that I forgot to eat), and the space to do whatever I needed to complete this book. I consider myself a lucky woman to have such a gracious and loving partner.

Thanks Mom, for living so long and so well.

And to Cheri Huber and the monks, deep gasshó for the love, patience, and compassion you so willingly offered to one who struggled so.

Awakening to a Fresh Perspective

I AM A BOOMER, PROUD to be part of a movement of amazing women who are redefining what it means to age well.

I am not a celebrity. I cook my own meals, drive my own car, choose my own clothes and do my own hair and makeup. I have an ex (two, to be exact), a (grown-up) blended family and a hubby. Probably like many of you.

The dirt really hit the fan when I decided to allow my hair to go silver. Life without hair dye brought me face to face with many of my fears, anxieties and limiting beliefs about entering my… *(gulp)* senior years.

Like so many women who have spent a lifetime marinating in our culture of youth and beauty and its negative stereotypes about aging, I secretly feared that I would eventually become a feeble, lonely, prune-faced, housebound, forgetful, sexless old woman with her boobs in her lap… and I was nothing less than *horrified* at the prospect. Having put too much value on the external aspects of my life, my physical appearance, my career and my *stuff,* I wondered who would I be as these things began to change.

I decided that rather than succumb to my limiting beliefs and fears about aging, I would challenge them by holding them up to the light of day. Where did they come from? Were they *true*? How could I change them? How freeing it was to eventually see that so much of what dampened my joy were really just the noisy voices of my past programming. It was also humbling to see how hard they were to silence. And so I dug in.

Little by little, I peeled away the leftovers of a life gone by. Like Michelangelo "releasing" a sculpture from a block of stone by chipping away the excess, so I approached my life—chipping away the old beliefs and fears that disguised my true essence. In the process, my own masterpiece began to emerge.

As I worked through my fears, it suddenly dawned on me—this was not the end of my life, but a *new beginning!* This was an opportunity to view life from a new vantage point and embrace a fresh perspective. It was a chance to reclaim the authentic me and design the life I want to live from here on out. By keeping the aspects of myself and my life that reflect *who I really am*, and changing, transforming or dropping those that don't, I could create the identity and life that I chose.

And thus I joined the ranks of the Amazing Grays, women of a certain age who understand that *we* are in charge of our experience of the aging process—not society, not the media and certainly not our programming about what it means to "get old." Rather than dread the coming years, we have decided to live our lives full out and unencumbered by our past.

This is a time in our lives when we get to be who we were meant to be. Who we choose to be. Sure, our bodies look a little worse for wear, but consider what we've been through! Adolescence, injury, childbirth, parenthood, loss, passion, heartbreak, wild sex, accidents, marriage, and more (not in any particular order). Consider yourself lucky for having made it this far—and for living at a time when we have so many advantages in health, technology, and education that allow us to be proactive in the aging process.

For you, it may not be the color of your hair that starts this internal process. It could be the changes in your body and face, the wrinkles and rolls that get harder to cover and ignore. It might be the changing landscape of your home and family as children move away (or back in) and have children of their own. Or you might find yourself looking at life in a new light as your career either comes to a close or becomes unfulfilling. For most of us, it's a sweet, scary, anxious and exciting time of life!

As I felt my way through the sea of emotions that arose on my own journey, I spoke with many women who were going through similar challenges. Most were grateful to be able to talk about what they were experiencing and breathed a huge sigh of relief knowing that they were not alone.

Despite our commonality, coming to terms with one's aging is a highly personal process that requires each of us to tap into our inner wisdom, trust our own experience, and draw our own conclusions. There are many opportunities throughout this book for you to write down your thoughts, experiences and insights. Writing has a way of prodding the unconscious to release the gifts it's been keeping safe for you. You might be surprised by what you uncover.

As you read this book, please remember that I have not "arrived." While I've made peace with much of my experience, I have yet to achieve total acceptance of the changes happening to my body (without my consent!). Sometimes, I am genuinely startled to see a silver haired woman reflected in my mirror. *Who is that? This wasn't supposed to happen!*

How our bodies age is determined by so many variables—genetics, sun damage, hormones, diet, smoking, exercise, attitude and more. We can't do anything about our heritage or how we treated our bodies in the past. But we can accept where we are now, and dip into the deep well of available knowledge on how to take better care of ourselves going forward. We can spend less time on negative thoughts about how we don't measure up and choose to enjoy our lives (and ourselves!) more. We can embrace the truth that we are so much more than our bodies.

How our attitudes age is up to us. We each have the ability to challenge the perceptions, limiting beliefs and behaviors that hold us back, and make choices that help us live a joyful, more inspired life.

By taking the focus off our packaging and redirecting it to our *essence*, we can see an aging body with a new clarity. While this body helps me function in the world, it certainly is not the essence of *who I am*.

In an effort to provide you with options (because we all have to find our own *answers*), this book explores the social, physical, psychological and spiritual perspectives on aging in the midst of our youth-obsessed culture. I read piles of books and articles, conferred with healthcare professionals and challenged the status quo. I learned about how our midlife hormones are there to rewire our brains, expand our worldview and help us give birth to our inner wise-woman. I experienced precious moments of grace, where I was offered the opportunity to step out of old identities, reawaken slumbering dreams, set clear boundaries, ask for what I wanted and challenge myself to try new things. Through it all, I realized it's not *that* we age that really matters—it's *how* we age.

This is not an anti-aging book. It's about living joyously—accepting and celebrating what we have been

Flexibility comes from having multiple choices; wisdom comes from having multiple perspectives.
ROBERT DILTS

given, and not wasting our time and energy trying to hang on to the past. It's about embracing a fresh start and creating the life you've always wanted, one that's in alignment with your deepest values and intentions and reflects the woman you've become.

Are you ready to join the ranks of Amazing Grays? No matter where you are on the continuum of life, you will find much to relate to in these pages (regardless of your hair color). Get ready to expose and discard your fears about growing older. Learn to challenge the behaviors that are keeping you stuck in a mindset of fear and limitation. Get ready to reawaken slumbering dreams and passions and try something new.

One variable we have absolute control over is our perspective. Therein lies our ability to age consciously and joyously.

We must alter our perspective, seeing things from a new place and therefore in a new way. Perspective creates perception, perception creates belief, belief creates behavior, behavior creates experience, and experience creates reality. If we want to change our reality, we need to change our perspective. We need to see things in a New Way.
    — NEALE DONALD WALSCH

How do you see things?
Is your life over—or did you save the best for last?

Epiphany

I REMEMBER THE DAY IT all changed for me: It was a sunny September afternoon and I was sitting in the hair salon. My head was soaked with hair dye and I had aluminum foil antennae poking out at odd angles; like everyone else, I was getting highlights too. I was doing my best not to inhale the awful smell as I waited out the processing time. It was an unpleasant but familiar ritual; I had endured these sessions for years.

At first, in my early forties, I plucked out those wiry gray hairs until my eyes watered. As they continued their march of domination through my soft brunette locks, and my do-it-yourself home coloring kits no longer did the trick, I started visiting the hairdresser every other month. Soon I found myself committed to the modern woman's ritual: the "smelly goop on the roots and scalp for 40 minutes, costs lots of money, and takes half a day every five to six weeks" ritual that so many of us have come to know so well.

A lot of us are pretty fed up with this routine, whether we admit it out loud or not. But, somehow, it just seems easier to keep making those appointments. And I did, for nearly 15 years.

Sometimes I didn't feel well after these trips to the salon. At first I just felt tired; then I graduated to dull headaches, nausea and swollen glands. Each time I felt this way, I told myself that I was just coming down with something. I didn't want to see that the timing of this "something" usually coincided with my hair appointment—because then I might have to do something about it! It's amazing how the mind will rationalize reality when it doesn't want to acknowledge the truth.

So there I was, sitting in the salon once more. My glands were puffing up and my stomach was mildly upset. My face held the grimace of a person changing a dirty diaper.

What happened next might sound a little bizarre. As I thumbed through my *O* magazine, I felt a sudden surge of energy spiral slowly through my body, beginning where I sit and rushing up, right out the top of my head. It was as if someone had just spun a feather duster through my very core and pulled it out the top of my head—whoosh! It was a full-body orgasm—and in public, no less! I glanced around to see if anyone else had noticed my wondrous experience, but everyone went about their business as usual.

I kept my head down and took a few deep breaths, turning my attention inward. What *was* that? I noticed a subtle, hard-to-describe shift inside me—like a physical experience of a mental *a-ha*, only I wasn't aware of any new insight… yet.

Then I looked in the mirror—really looked. Somebody looked back and with great passion, seemed to ask, *What are you doing?* I noticed my eyes widen, and while I had no answer to a question I wasn't even sure I understood, something deep inside me began to awaken in response.

Questions that had been lurking below my radar suddenly began to surface. *Why was I putting myself*

*through this? Who was I coloring my hair for? Was I willing
to risk getting sick? Maybe the term "hair dye" had a hidden
meaning? What was my fear of looking older? Who would I
be if I let my "silver lining" show? Would I still be attractive?
Why was it important to be attractive to others anyway
(other than my husband, whom I know would love me even
with a bag on my head)? Who decided that silver-haired
women are not attractive, desirable or sexy?*

As I continued to gaze in the mirror, seeing the smelly
black goop on my head, another realization softly crept
into my awareness. Each morning and evening, to help
temper my hot flashes and sleepless nights, I rubbed
a hormone cream directly onto my skin, where it was
absorbed into my bloodstream. Wait....

*I rubbed it onto my skin, where it was absorbed into my
bloodstream!*

If the hormones in the cream move through my skin
and into my bloodstream, what's stopping those toxic
chemicals that were marinating my scalp at that very
moment from doing the same?!

And there it was. I suddenly saw the connection I had
been denying: a direct correlation between the chemicals
on my head and the physical symptoms I experienced
whenever I colored my hair.

That woman in the mirror decided right then and
there that this was the last time she was going to color her
hair. *How* I was going to go from a chin-length brunette
(with those lovely golden highlights I was so attached to)
to my natural color was a complete mystery, but I knew it
was time.

Over the coming days and weeks, it slowly dawned
on me that this process of going gray had many layers,
and that perhaps, at age 55, I was finally embracing my
hard-earned maturity. Maybe, I surmised, it's okay to be
50-something? Could I embrace the lines on my face and

the new contours of my changing body? Could I accept myself as a mature woman and redefine what that means to me—not *old*… just not so young?

My choice was clear: I could cling to an outdated image of myself, or I could honor my new awareness and allow a new, *authentic* beauty to emerge.

This was the beginning of a bumpy journey that brought me face to face with many of the social, physical, psychological, and spiritual issues that often arise during major life transitions. Dealing with this new reality also gave rise to a range of emotions—anxiety, fear, resistance, curiosity, and ultimately the grace to accept.

By following an organic flow of questions and answers, I sifted through layers and layers of influence. The gems I uncovered in the process of going gray were deeper and richer than I could have imagined. It became a journey that brought me to levels of acceptance, clarity and understanding I had never known before.

The most important step in this amazing process was in fact the first: the recognition that I had a choice. I could choose to resent my age and hide any evidence that I'd slipped past 50, or I could choose to age gracefully and enjoy the ride.

Either way, I'm still getting older.

PART ONE

SOCIAL
PERSPECTIVES

What Aging Means to Us

*Always remember that it is your birthright and
natural state to be wise and noble,
loving and generous,
to esteem yourself and others,
to be creative and constantly renewing yourself,
to be engaged in the world in awe and depth,
to have courage and to rely on yourself,
to be joyous and effortlessly accomplished,
to be strong and effective,
to enjoy peace of mind and
to be present to the unfolding mystery of your life.*

THE WISDOM OF THE ENNEAGRAM
DON RISO AND RUSS HUDSON

What Aging Means to Us

AFTER SPENDING THE LAST SEVERAL DECADES in a Madison Avenue *cult*ure of youth and beauty, many of us are feeling uncertain of our place in a society that seems not to honor or appreciate the aging. Our roles are changing and we are beginning to question the time and energy we put into maintaining the look of our youth. We wonder:

> *Will I be invisible as I age? Will I be respected? Will I be loved? Why do my looks matter so much? What am I so afraid of? Who am I now that I'm no longer of reproductive age? Will I still be important? Will I be seen as a person of interest? Is everyone this scared of dying? I'm a Boomer... can't I do this my way?*

Thankfully, we boomers now have information available to us that has turned the whole notion of what it means to age on its head! True to our history, we'll continue to make it up as we go along, testing the waters and pushing into new possibilities.

One thing for certain is that whatever we counted on to define us in the past will change in the future. Appearance, talent, roles, responsibilities—it *all* changes. Resisting change—trying to hold on to what was—is like holding your breath and hoping you'll eventually get your way. It just doesn't work.

We have come to a crossroads, and the direction that each of us chooses to take will determine how we experience the rest of our life.

Rather than sit back and allow our fears of aging to determine our experience of aging, let's take hold of the wheel and steer ourselves toward a new reality, one that supports us in being vibrant, active and engaged members of society. Rather than hide away any evidence of our years, we can shift our focus to a more authentic and joyful way to age: with grace and intention... and gusto!

It's a scary, sweet, and exciting time of life; an opportunity to redefine who you are *now*, and decide...

Who will I become?

CHAPTER 1

Young...Forever?

SHHHH… LISTEN. DO YOU hear it? It's the shrill cry of millions of baby-boomer women looking in the mirror and wondering, "Hey, what's going on here? When did I get this roll around my middle? Where did *that* wrinkle come from? Do I see *another* gray hair? I'm too young for this! This must be a mistake! Stop this nonsense! This wasn't supposed to happen! Not to *me*!" We are the generation that vowed to stay forever young—and now we're facing the reality that we were… *wrong*.

I can relate. One minute I was 30, the next I'm pushing 60! As a woman on the leading edge of the baby-boom generation, I still carry a set of beliefs and expectations that were shaped by our generation's denial that our good life could come to an end. We'll never get old—we'll get better! Somehow we expected a major breakthrough in medical science that would fix all that ails us so we could live happily and healthfully into our hundreds.

As the years pass and it gradually sinks in that this miracle fix is still beyond our reach, I notice there is even

Inside every older person is a younger person wondering what happened.
JENNIFER YANE

a little anger simmering just below the surface. *This wasn't supposed to happen!*

There are a lot of us. The oldest baby boomers turned 60 in 2006; the youngest were 42. Seventy-six *million* of us were born between 1946 and 1964, the official bookends of the baby-boom generation. Because of this 18-year expanse of time, the boomer generation is divided into leading-edge boomers, born between 1946 and 1955, and trailing-edge boomers born from 1956 to 1964. Coming of age at the time of Kennedy's Camelot was very different from growing up amidst the Iran-Contra Scandal and the Reagan years, and these early influences differentiated us in ways we're still discovering. Early boomers and late boomers may be nearly a generation apart, but the one thing we have in common is that we're all getting older... and we're all starting to explore what that means—to *us*.

It all began with the swiveling hips of Elvis, the *yeah yeah yeah* of the mop-topped Beatles and the great revolution that was Rock 'n' Roll. As a generation, we pushed the envelope, both socially and politically. Some of us experimented with outrageous fashions, mind-altering substances and political dissidence; some of us toed the line. Because of our sheer numbers, we cascaded through the years with glacial force, altering the landscape of American society forever.

Baby boomers were the first generation to define our selves as distinct from our parents and create a culture of our own. According to a feature article in *Newsweek* magazine, we "invented not just the epiphenomena of youth culture—blue jeans and rock music, sexual permissiveness and political alienation—but the very idea of youth as a separate realm of experience and knowledge."[1]

Now, our generation's first cultural contribution—establishing youth as its own distinct culture—is coming back to bite us! Millions of baby boomers who saw themselves as integral to the radical youth culture of yesteryear are now struggling to let go and swallow a very hard truth: *it's another generation's turn to set the standards.*

This youth-driven culture has not only survived and thrived, but has become a driving force in our economy and left profound changes on our social and moral values. The current generation of youth has the powerful voice of a worldwide media at its fingertips, with the ability to determine what's *in* and what's *out*. Billions of advertising dollars and countless hours of media time target the fast-paced, waste-no-time, take-no-prisoners, technologically driven youth culture, leaving many of us choking on their dust.

Perhaps for the first time in our lives, the leading-edge baby boomers are on the *out* list, and we don't know how to handle it. (As for you trailing-edge boomers, just wait—your turn is coming.)

Rather than accept our changing role, many of us try to emulate the younger generation. You'll have to agree, it's not a pretty picture. (Ladies, just because we wore low-slung hip-hugger jeans to Woodstock doesn't mean we can pull them off now!) Trying to cling to time as it rushes past you is not only futile—it will give you whiplash! And it only leads to more insecurity.

Boomers are facing a wide array of questions about our rights, roles and responsibilities. Whether your music idols were the Beatles or the Bee Gees, we're the generation that is going to break it down, sort it out, and claim the joyful vitality that seemed to elude previous generations as they aged. We're redefining the aging process—our new frontier!

In the 60s, people took acid to make the world weird. Now the world is weird and people take Prozac to make it normal.

UNKNOWN

It's Not Your Mother's Old Age

Rest assured, we will *never* be the "senior citizens" of generations past. We'll make bifocals hip, create fashions that focus on comfort *and* style, and still be rock 'n' rolling at our 75th birthday parties.

While our parents' generation typically followed a linear life path—from school to marriage to children, or from school to career to retirement—our generation is completely unpredictable. It's hard to know what stage of life boomers are in just by knowing our age. We tend to reinvent ourselves and reorganize our lives every three to five years.[2] We might start college at 50 or a new career at 60. A boomer could be a new parent, a grandparent, or both at the same time.

The social freedoms that many young women take for granted today were crafted on the shoulders of the young men and women of the 1960s and 1970s who stood up and said, "We won't take anymore." I was one of those women who came of age in the 1960s, metaphorically burning my bra and protesting social inequities to the tunes of Jimi Hendrix and Janis Joplin. We asked for respect, demanded to be heard and pushed against barriers of age, race and gender. We built our collective identity by questioning the wisdom and authority of our elders. As a generation we wore the mantle of anti-everything establishment and took great pride in doing things differently from those who came before us.

The irony is that, as we aged, our counterculture mentality evolved and slowly became the prevailing culture. According to David Brooks, author of *Bobos in Paradise*, "Bohemian attitudes from the hippie 1960s have merged with the bourgeois attitudes of the yuppie 1980s to form a new culture, which is a synthesis of the two. … The people who dominate our culture now are richer and

True terror is to wake up one morning and discover that your high school class is running the country.

KURT VONNEGUT

more worldly than the hippies, but more spiritualized than the stereotypical yuppies."[3]

Many of us professed not to need fancy cars and houses and all the excess trappings of a capitalist society. Then we grew up and wanted lots of stuff, and many of us bought in to the system, hook, line and sinker. We moved to the suburbs, bought homes, drove gas-guzzling cars and sent our kids to the best schools we could find. To ease our consciences, many of us redefined our sense of social responsibility. We drive gas-guzzlers but we give to Greenpeace. We buy prepackaged gourmet foods but support the local food bank. We buy designer clothing, but we give our rejects—sometimes with the price tag still attached—to the Salvation Army.

So it should come as no surprise that we are also redefining what it means to age well. Aging used to be perceived as simply the deterioration of youth and vitality. The stereotypical image of frail old folks drooling into their applesauce kept all of us in such fear that denial seemed a welcome relief. Now that the boomers are turning gray, we're on a collective mission to challenge the stereotypes.

You're never too old to become younger.
MAE WEST

Baby boomers tend to embody a heady concoction of entitlement, moxie, imagination and spirituality, tempered with just enough insight to give us the voice we need to redefine the aging process into one that suits us. To us, age isn't a number—it's a state of mind.

A paradigm shift is occurring. To paraphrase Dylan Thomas, "We will not go gentle into that good night." *No way!* We're going to make this journey over to our liking. Once again, we're going to do it our way.

The truth is that our finest moments are most likely to occur when we are feeling deeply uncomfortable, unhappy, or unfulfilled. For it is only in such moments, propelled by our discomfort, that we are likely to step out of our ruts and start searching for different ways or truer answers.
M. SCOTT PECK

When Do We Become Old?

Remember the days when we refused to trust anyone over 30? Thirty seemed so *ancient*! Now 60 seems pretty young to me. "Old" seems to apply to people in their 90s, don't you think? (Ask me again when I'm 80.) I just want to stay as old as I feel—which certainly isn't as old as I am. While my outsides may define me differently, inside—I still feel 30. How old do you feel?

Breakthroughs in science, medicine and technology are making it possible to live longer and healthier lives. At the beginning of the 20th century, the average life expectancy in the United States was about 50 years. Today, it's close to 77 and rising. As a few resilient folks have proven, people can now live more than 115 years! According to the latest life expectancy data, most women over 60 can plan on living another 20 years or more. (Ha! They haven't factored in the Amazing Grays yet!)

The great secret that all old people share is that you really haven't changed in seventy or eighty years. Your body changes, but you don't change at all. And that, of course, causes great confusion.

DORIS LESSING

Stop for a moment and ask yourself:

~ How old were you 25 years ago?

~ What year was it?

~ What significant events have occurred in the 25 years between then and now? Think about trips, vacations, holidays, celebrations, births, deaths, marriage, divorce, and relocation.

Now, close your eyes and reflect on the life you have lived, all the love you have given and received, all the places you've been, all the chocolate you've eaten in the years since then—and know that you likely have at least that much life ahead of you! Now there's a comforting perspective. We each have an opportunity to use the wisdom and power garnered over the last 50 years to redefine what the next 50 will look like.

While we all have to age, we don't have to get *old*. Most of our lives are spent growing and developing. We engage in new experiences, challenge old beliefs, and remain curious and open to what life has to offer. When we stop growing, developing, and being curious and open, when our beliefs and attitudes become fixed and we lose the zest for life, we get stuck in a rut. Our lives become predictable, uneventful and focused on the past. This stagnation is what makes us *old*.

We do have a choice. Fewer and fewer of us are opting for traditional "retirement." The golden years are no longer about rocking chairs and television—they're about reinvention and re-engaging with long-neglected dreams and aspirations. It can be a time to travel, begin new careers, socialize, go on adventures, tend your hobbies and nurture deeper connections with loved ones. For many, the second half of life has also become a time to build one's legacy: to give back to the world and make things better for the next generation.

I found that as I aged, *doing good* became more important than *looking good*. I had enough stuff. I was moved to express my authenticity, deepen my spirituality, and challenge the beliefs that kept me contained and my personal world small. It seemed more important than ever to fill my life with the people, experiences and adventures that engage me and encourage me to live fully and authentically, so I can live the rest of my years with more gusto, passion, and curiosity than I've ever known before.

As I aged, I became less interested in pleasing others and more committed to honoring myself. I realized I had the option to live the rest of my life *without* all the self-doubt, hesitancy and second-guessing that I tormented myself with during the first half.

In conversations with a number of women, I discovered that it was right around their mid-fifties when many

When one door closes, another opens. But, we so often look so long upon the closed door—that we do not see the one which has been opened for us.
ALEXANDER GRAHAM BELL

of them begin to seriously question and challenge the need to adhere to standards that no longer supported them in living fulfilling lives. Many referred to it as a midlife speed-bump! This seems to be the age juncture where many women choose to slow down, reassess their priorities, turn up the heat under a simmering passion, allow their hair to go natural or make any number of choices that support them in living more authentically.

It wasn't until I had my salon epiphany (at age 55) that I really began to look at my life through fresh eyes. I finally stepped out of the perpetual "self-improvement" loop and started to ask some serious questions. *Why was I so invested in looking youthful? What was I really afraid of? What would happen if I stopped? Who am I **now**?*

Living in a culture of distraction, it's easy to gloss over what's really important. We know the importance of slowing down, but few of us do. Sometimes life has to shake us up to remind us how important it is to sink into the stillness and listen. My "salon epiphany" encouraged me to pay attention, and the answers slowly surfaced.

Bubbling just below my conscious awareness was a potent layer of beliefs and fears about aging, messages that influenced so many of my thoughts, feelings and actions. *Old people don't matter. Gray-haired women are not attractive. This is the beginning of the end.* Unexamined, these beliefs and fears were dictating my experience and stirring up a low-level anxiety about what was to come as I aged.

It finally occurred to me that the energy necessary to hold these fears at bay was probably far greater than the energy it would take to make peace with them, once and for all. Rather than spend my time, energy and money trying to *override* Mother Nature, I wondered if it might be better spent on *embracing* Mother Nature. Perhaps it might be more useful to focus on the things I could do something about, and let go of the rest.

I reminded myself once again that I could face the next step kicking and screaming, or approach it with grace. I did a lot of both. Actually, I still do a lot of both. Going gray was relatively easy; it's the graceful part that I struggle with.

CHAPTER 2

What if It Really Is All in Our Heads?

Q UANTUM PHYSICS IS TURNING Darwinian science on its head, saying our physical reality is moldable, created from the inside out. It suggests we are not solid matter, but simply energy, vibrating at different frequencies. Quantum physics maintains that our thoughts become the energetic beacons we send out into the world, communicating what we expect. If you order scrambled eggs and toast at a restaurant, you expect to get scrambled eggs and toast. Our thoughts are like "orders" we place to the universe—and we generally get what we ask for. Unfortunately for many of us, much of what we believe (and therefore think) is directed by our unconscious mind. For example, if we've been programmed to believe that aging means "frail, unimportant and unloved," we unconsciously expect and will likely experience that reality as we age. If we challenge that belief and instead order "empowered, fit, energized and self-sufficient," *that's* what we're likely to receive, assuming we have also taken the action necessary to support our

As he thinketh in
his heart, so is he.

PROVERBS 23:7

desire. Truth is, no matter how much you *want* to be fit, you'll never *be* fit if you're just parking yourself in a comfy chair and eating bon bons. (Regardless of how many butt squeezes you do!)

In her classic book, *Mindfulness*, Dr. Ellen Langer writes,

> The regular and "irreversible" cycles of aging that we witness in the later stages of human life may be a product of certain assumptions about how one is supposed to grow old. If we didn't feel compelled to carry out these limiting mindsets, we might have a greater chance of replacing years of decline with years of growth and purpose.[4]

Wow!

She suggests that how we *think* about aging will affect how we *experience* aging, supporting the scientific notion that energy follows thought. You may have heard it expressed in other ways: *What you think about, you bring about. Whatever you focus on expands. The quality of your life will be determined by the focus of your attention.* These statements all point to a basic principle: our reality will be influenced by our thoughts and beliefs—both conscious and unconscious—and the actions we take to support them.

*Life consists of what
a man is thinking of
all day.*

RALPH WALDO
EMERSON

Much of what we believe about aging is based on old programming. These beliefs then create fears that manifest as dire warnings about all the awful things that could happen to us if we're not vigilant about maintaining prevailing cultural standards of youth and beauty. No wonder we're frightened when we see the signs of aging catching up with us!

Fear is caused by the stories we make up in our heads—about everything! It's our belief about something and the meaning we give it that generates a fearful feeling.

Ultimately, all that really matters when one thinks about gray hair, wrinkles or a rounder figure is what those details *mean* to you. For instance, I noticed that gray hair, in and of itself, is nothing to be afraid of. It didn't hurt, or say nasty things to me, or feel physically different than any other color of hair. It's what my mind did with the idea of gray hair, and the meaning I assigned to gray hair, that struck terror in my heart: *I'll be old, unattractive, invisible, unimportant.* If I believed these associations to be real and true, and didn't stop to challenge them, they would have controlled my experience, and I might still be dyeing my hair!

False Evidence Appearing Real[5]

"The only thing we have to fear is fear itself—nameless, unreasoning, unjustified terror which paralyzes needed efforts to convert retreat into advance." These wise words from Franklin D. Roosevelt point us toward a profound truth—fear is the enemy (and, I would add—*especially* when it comes to aging). While you are most likely familiar with the first part of that quote, it's the latter that best describes what happens to us when we allow our beliefs to go unchallenged. How can we move gracefully into the rest of our life when our unbounded fears of aging paralyze our efforts and keep us retreating while trying to hold on to who we were? For most of us, it's these unconscious and unexamined fears that keep us from experiencing the life we truly want. Anxiety fills the space between what was and what we believe is coming.

Many of us are looking at our senior years through a lens that is clouded by fear. As we disengage from the roles we played in our younger years and begin to explore other options, we're likely to experience a certain degree of discomfort. In addition to the uncertainty of feeling out a new role, our deep-seated fears about aging will surface. Instead of letting them haunt you, explore this framework of beliefs and fears—knowing they will boomerang right back as your reality if you allow them to fester.

I've noticed that most of the things in life that frighten me are maintained by the absence of scrutiny. Once I move them out of the periphery and into full view, it becomes possible to tear down the self-limiting beliefs and fears that control me and replace them with the perspectives and beliefs I *choose*. In other words, before I can consciously create a fresh start, I need to explore what I've been expecting (and unknowingly asking for).

In order to gray gracefully and arrive at a place of joy and acceptance, I needed to confront the negative fears and beliefs I held about aging—and consciously order up something different. I invite you to do the same.

When it comes to staying young, a mind-lift beats a face-lift any day.
MARTY BUCELLA

Take a few minutes and explore your fears of aging.

~ Picture yourself 10 or 20 years into the future, and start brainstorming a list of questions, fears or negative beliefs you have about getting or looking older. As I examined my fears, they seemed to revolve around three key issues:

Irrelevance and loss of love:

Will I continue to matter? Will I be seen as attractive? Desirable? Loved for who I am? Will I be invisible? Will others still see me as a person of interest? Will I be respected? Will I become just a part of the wallpaper in a youth-oriented society? Old people are not attractive people. No one wants to hear from an old person.

Safety and security:

Will I be physically safe? Financially secure? Will I be able to take care of myself? What if no one will hire me? Will I end up a bag lady? What if I

*become mentally or physically infirm? Will I end
up in a nursing home? What if my partner dies
before I do? Who will watch over me? How will I
keep fit? I'm afraid to be alone.*

Life's meaning and purpose:

*Have I done what I came here to do? What's it
really all about? I'm afraid of dying. Have I made
a difference? How can I continue to make a
difference? I missed my window of opportunity. If
I haven't done what I came to do by now, it's too
late for me.*

~ Underline any of the examples above that apply
to you, and continue to add your own fears and
concerns to the list. Take your time with this; dig
up every underlying concern you have. Don't edit
or judge the things that come up—just allow them
to surface and write them down. Revealing them
to the light of day could be exactly what you need
in order to gain the clarity to move beyond them.

_____

_____

_____

_____

_____

_____

Is this the mindset you choose to support? In the
face of these limiting beliefs and the fears they create,
it's no wonder we want to hold on to those aspects of
ourselves that have provided us with a sense of importance, inclusion and attention for most of our lives: our
looks, our careers and our roles as mother, spouse, and/
or career woman. As we redefine what it means to be a

mature member of society, watching for these fears and confronting them head-on is the only way to ensure they don't have the power to determine our experience. If we accept these thoughts as *true*, we're more likely to live in a constant state of anxiety, which leads to a high level of stress—which is likely to cut short the life we have.

Understanding the genesis of our fears and the process that holds them in place can help us put them to rest.

Don't Believe Everything You Think

Just because you think it, doesn't mean it's true. The thoughts that float through your head, and the fears that grow from them, actually have very little basis in reality. They stem from a lifetime of conditioning—all the things we were taught to believe as we grew up. While some are useful, most are not. It's only by challenging these beliefs that we can choose another perspective.

Our conditioning is maintained by our inner voices. While the inner voices will profess to try and keep us safe, it's helpful to understand that these fears are a defense mechanism. What are they defending? A basic need.

According to Maslow's "Hierarchy of Needs," we all have four basic needs that assert themselves in a linear progression. Our four most basic needs are: 1) food and shelter; 2) safety and security; 3) love and approval; and 4) esteem. The second-level need (safety and security) is not felt until the more powerful first-level need has been met, and the third-level need will not be experienced until the second-level is satisfied, and so on.

Once the first four levels are met, a person moves on to explore higher levels of self-actualization and transcendence. These higher states of being instill a zest for life, calmness and serenity, joy, and an overall confidence in one's ability to handle whatever challenges life presents.[6]

As we willingly enter each place of fear, each place of deficiency and insecurity in ourselves, we will discover that its walls are made of untruths, of old images of ourselves, of ancient fears, of false ideas of what is pure and what is not.

JACK KORNFIELD

This is the state of actualization many of us yearn for as we grow older. As we mature, many of us are able to meet our four basic needs most of the time and have moved on to enrich our lives through higher levels of self-actualization.

However, as circumstances change (job loss, divorce, *aging*, death of a loved one, natural disaster, civil unrest, etc.) and the things or conditions that meet our essential needs are threatened, we often shift our attention back to fulfilling those basic needs, setting aside the pursuit of our higher needs for self-actualization and transcendence.

When your basic needs are threatened, your mind generates fearful thoughts, stemming from a sense of self-preservation. They aren't necessarily true; they're just mental red flags telling you to pay attention and protect that basic need. Unfortunately, most of us believe these fearful thoughts to be true, giving them the power to stop us in our tracks.

It's hard to be graceful when you feel like you are fighting for your life. Without realizing it, many of us turn over a lot of our precious time and energy to dealing with perceived threats—*perceived* being the key word here. Once you change your perception, the fear often vanishes.

Challenge your fearful thoughts! Some of our fears are driven by valid concerns and deeply held cultural beliefs; others are not. There is no easy fix, but often just naming the fear can dilute some of its power. Remember, in most cases, our basic needs are not really being threatened… we just *think* they are. If we take our thoughts at face value and don't look beyond them, we experience a sense of dissatisfaction or suffering. I've learned that any time I feel unhappy, afraid, dissatisfied or miserable, I am identified with or attached to a fearful thought. Recycling these thoughts over and over in my mind is like being on a treadmill, using up my time and energy—but never getting me anywhere.

We behave and perform in life not in accordance with reality but in accordance with our perception of reality.
UNKNOWN

Turning towards the Future without Hanging On to the Past

The good news is that there are useful tools to help us disengage from these fearful voices in our heads, leaving us free to fully engage in creating the life we choose.

Revisit the list of fears you constructed on page 19. For each belief or fear you wrote down, ask yourself: *Is it true? How do I know? Who said so? Does carrying this fear or belief support me or keep me from living a fulfilling life? What's the worst that can happen?*

~ Take the time to journal your responses.

_____

_____

_____

_____

~ Read over your list of fears and highlight those you can actually **do** something about now. Then, figure out what action you might take to improve the situation or set your mind at ease. For example:

- If you fear infirmity, put a plan in place to ensure how you will be cared for if you do face that situation. Join a gym or hire a personal trainer to help get your body into shape, and take steps to eat more healthfully.

- If you fear destitution, talk to a financial planner, take steps to put aside money, generate more income or find a roommate to share expenses. If you are currently in a partnership, be sure you know where important documents are kept, what your financial status is, and where all the assets are. Get a credit card issued in your own name.

- If you fear being alone, build relationships and engage in more activities.
- If you fear losing control of your affairs, take the time to legally put in place how you want your assets dispersed and to whom, unless you wish to leave the government in charge of disposing of your assets and taxing them to the max. (You don't want that—trust me.) Depending on your state laws, a Revocable Living Trust can help protect your estate.
- If you fear your wishes will not be respected, be sure to put a Health Directive in place. You can leave clear instructions on who will become your advocate if you become infirm, when to pull the plug, and what to do with your remains. Once you become sick or indisposed, it's too late; the state assigns a conservator to your case and gives them the power to spend your money and decide what is best for you. (You *really* don't want that.)

I know, I know… these are not easy things to think about. I recently went through this process, and while it was difficult, I now feel free of some nagging fears that were undermining my sense of well-being. My instructions will sit in the lockbox for another 50 years—and I no longer have to think about them. Ignoring the fact that your body and assets will not be going with you is not a useful strategy. Honor yourself (and your heirs) by being a good steward and taking care of your business. Then get on with the business of living well.

Nothing conquers fear like action. The point is to bring your fears of aging into conscious awareness so they are not running the show from backstage. By putting a plan in place, taking care of our affairs, and keeping ourselves healthy and fit, we can recover the energy we lost to fear and use it to live life to the fullest.

But what about the fears we *can't* do anything about? Trying to rationally deal with an irrational fear or belief is like trying to stuff a huge rubber pillow into a tiny little purse… it just doesn't work. Irrational fears sometimes need irrational solutions. If there is no action you can take to mitigate a fear, it is probably the result of an overactive imagination that's running on old programming. Your inner voices will taunt you and wrinkle up your insides, threatening you with all the awful things that *might* happen as you get older. None of us knows what the future holds. Worrying about things you have no control over is simply suffering in advance. And remember, latching on to these fears will often draw to you the very thing you are afraid of!

So how do we handle these fears? And who is it that keeps spouting all these irrational concerns anyway?

About those voices

You can't have made it this far in life without becoming aware of the cacophony of voices in your head. They tell us we're not good enough, not smart enough, not doing it right, not measuring up. They second-guess our best efforts, creating doubt and stress. They are the voices that tell us to do something and then beat us up for doing it! They maintain an internal dialogue of self-hate, poisoning us against ourselves. They constantly remind us of all the bad things that could happen, and keep us immobilized with fear and recrimination. It's these inner voices that keep us stuck in fear and resistance and don't allow us to open up to accepting new possibilities. What they have to say is cruel, untrue, and repetitive—and has nothing to do with who we really are!

Train yourself to let go of everything you fear to lose.

JEDI MASTER YODA

There is no "winning" against these voices; there is only "not believing" them. When you hear the voices in your head whining about all the awful things that will happen as you get older, I suggest you not take them so seriously. Just nod your head, agree with them, and move on.

Agree with them? What?!

This may seem contrary to what you've been taught, but it's *one* way to regain your peace of mind. Dealing with the negative inner voices of our conditioning is a life-long process, and simply agreeing with them can be a useful tool in your arsenal, and a place to begin. It seems illogical, but when you agree with the internal voices of negativity and fear, they lose their power. They have nowhere to go, nothing to do. By paying them no attention and brushing them off with a simple "uh-huh," you don't allow the negative beliefs to take root.

Agree with them, yes. *Believe* them, no. There is a big difference between agreeing and believing. Here's how that works:

If another person criticizes your cooking, organization skills, memory, lack of exercise, etc., and you argue with them, what happens? The conversation typically escalates into a right vs. wrong argument; you spend enormous amounts of energy defending yourself, and everyone walks away feeling angry and self-righteous. By simply *agreeing* with the other person's criticism, you take the steam out of their argument. At first they might look at you with suspicion, wondering what you are up to. They may even try to bait you with more negativity. If you don't buy into it and you simply say "uh-huh" and move on, they'll (eventually) drop it. What they're looking for is your reaction and the sense of power they feel in controlling your reactions. The same is true for the voices of your conditioning.

Don't argue with your inner voices. It only starts a back-and-forth conversation that is too exhausting to engage in. Simply acknowledge whatever the voice says, and move on. You know the real truth—that you are wonderful, wise, beautiful, and authentic. (Don't you?)

"Gray hair is dowdy." Uh-huh.
"You'll be invisible." Uh-huh.
"No one will find you attractive." Uh-huh.

Sounds simple, but it's not easy. For a while I had "uh-huh" sticky notes all around my house, reminding me not to believe the voices. As long as I remember to practice saying "uh-huh," I'm freer, happier, and more authentic with each passing day.

Truly, the most toxic relationship most of us are in is the one we have with ourselves. In this way we're all victims of abuse—*inner* abuse! Do you hear that voice in your head right now, telling you this is too simple and will not work? What do you say?

Uh-huh.

Many of life's greatest gifts are cloaked in simplicity.

Reassure Yourself

I found that by raising my awareness of what passes through my mind, I am able to steadily change how I see—and therefore experience—the world. Somehow, the light of awareness gradually deflates negative thoughts, and I am slowly transformed. Tapping into the wisdom within, I am able to counter the poisonous voices of self-hate with messages that reassure me of a more gracious reality. This is clearly a lifelong process requiring attention and practice.

Once I uncovered what I'd been unconsciously expecting and became clear on what I *don't* want—the question then became, "What *do* I want the second half of my life to look like?" Which qualities support me in being happy, productive, physically fit and financially solvent? What might they be for you?

Which thoughts or beliefs would support you being more powerful and authentic as you become the beautiful sage you were meant to be?

$\sim$ Jot down your responses.

Examples:

Age has nothing to do with my beauty, which emanates from within.

I continue to make a difference in the world simply by showing up authentically, as I am.

By living every moment fully, I have an opportunity to be a positive example to my children, grand-children, family, friends, community, etc.

My powerful presence and love of self draw people to me.

Aging is a privilege for which I am grateful.

My body is strong and fit and my actions support me in maintaining my health.

I say yes to what life offers me.

_____

_____

_____

_____

Keep these reassurances in front of you. They are not affirmations of what you would *like* to be true. They are a reassurance of what is *already* true—you just have to claim it. These are the kind of thoughts that will support you in accepting and embracing a fresh perspective as you move into this next phase of your life. We are truly blessed

The thought manifests as the word; the word manifests as the deed; the deed develops into habit; and habit hardens into character. So watch the thought and its ways with care, and let it spring from love born out of concern for all beings.
GAUTAMA BUDDHA

when we finally understand that we each have the power and the ability to choose our own experience. By challenging our perceptions, we can create empowering beliefs that allow us to behave in ways that support us in living in integrity with our deepest wishes.

When fearful or distressing thoughts overwhelm your mind, give them the ol' uh-huh and reassure yourself with positive messages. In the process, you'll be claiming the reality you *choose*.

So, I wondered, what stops us from choosing to live with gusto and embracing the joys of life, especially as we age? Looking around me at the abundance of media that constantly bombard us with images of the ideal life and the perfect look, it became clear. Identifying too closely with our culture of materialism, paired with the limiting fears and beliefs that go hand in hand with trying to measure up to unrealistic standards, can literally drain the juice right out of you!

Even after all these years, I *still* find myself caught in the habit of comparison. While I understand intellectually that my age, the size and firmness of my body, the smoothness of my face, and the color of my hair have no relevance to who I am as a person, I find myself measuring what I actually look like against what I'm *supposed* to look like: the perfect young woman as depicted by various media representations.

It's an old habit. In my thirties and forties I focused, with varying degrees of success, on overriding Mother Nature. I took steps to try to stop the effects of time. I was often on the lookout for the next product, garment or exercise program that would help me hang on to the image of what I thought I should look like, based on what the popular culture was touting at the time. It's an exhausting process. Why, I wondered, was I so reluctant to embrace my age?

Taking joy in life is a woman's best cosmetic.
ROSALIND RUSSELL

CHAPTER 3

The Culture Made Me Do It

A S I APPROACHED THE Big 5-0, I wrestled with a deluge of questions and self-doubts. Like a lot of women, hitting this half-century marker inspired a determined effort to prove that I could still maintain the look of my youth. I loved hearing people say, "You're 50? You look great! I would never guess you're that old!" (Is a backhanded compliment better than no compliment?)

Maintaining a youthful appearance took on a renewed focus, and I spent more time, energy and money trying to keep things as they had been, to no avail. My body just didn't respond as it had before. Frankly, I hadn't counted on things morphing quite so quickly!

It was eye-opening to contemplate just how much time, energy, and money I've spent during my lifetime trying to look younger or different than I am. For what? For whom? More importantly—do I want to continue spending my time, energy and money that way? Do you?

For each person in the world, much of what we believe to be right and good and true is learned from the *cul*ture

The process of maturing is an art to be learned, an effort to be sustained. By the age of fifty you have made yourself what you are, and if it is good, it is better than your youth.
MARYA MANNES

29

we are born into. Simply stated, culture is a shared set of ideas about reality—right and wrong, good and bad, standards, beliefs, rules and expectations about "how we do things here." It's shocking to realize how much power a culture has over people.

In Western society, the intense glamorization of youth and beauty distorts our perception of reality. It would appear that every age and ethnicity has its secret demons. If it's not about the effects of aging, it's the texture of their hair, the size of their butt, their depth of skin tone, or the lack of a crease in the eyelid. It seems very few of us are simply okay with who we are and how we look! For many, it feeds a lifelong struggle with self-esteem. Women everywhere feel not good enough as we struggle to meet an unachievable standard: impeccably dressed, impressively addressed, and perfectly shaped. As the effects of aging start to appear—rounder figures, wrinkled skin and thinner hair—these feelings only get worse and many of us feel marginalized, insecure, even self-loathing.

In a *Glamour* magazine survey, 61 percent of respondents said they were *ashamed* of their hips, 64 percent were *ashamed* of their stomachs and 72 percent were *ashamed* of their thighs (emphasis added).[7]

Shame is an emotion that combines feelings of dishonor, unworthiness and embarrassment. Over two-thirds of women surveyed feel *shame* about the way their bodies look! Dishonored. Unworthy. Embarrassed. We've been so conditioned about the way we *should* look that we feel like failures, as though we've let someone down, if we don't meet those standards.

It seems people everywhere are driven to fulfill a basic human need: wanting to fit in, measure up, and be "good enough" to be loved and accepted. Our glamorous, stylized North American culture offers to fulfill this need for women by suggesting that we can be

What we see depends mainly on what we look for.
JOHN LUBBOCK

loved and accepted *if* we adhere to the current cultural standard of looking young and beautiful. Following this line of thinking, the belief becomes: "*If* I look young and beautiful, *then* I will be loved and accepted. If I don't fulfill this standard, then I will be rejected and unloved and 'not good enough.'" Since only a small fraction of women ever come close to meeting these standards, many of us end up feeling there is something wrong with us!

Given that option, it's no wonder many of us are willing to forgo our better judgment and do whatever it takes to maintain these often unrealistic standards—surgery, Botox, hair dye, dermabrasion. Some studies suggest that women become less obsessed with media images and more content with their bodies as they age, but for many of us, it's a long haul. We get stuck in the illusion of not good enough and struggle to release media-constructed concepts of how a woman *should* look.

As we become older and no longer meet the prevailing standards of young and beautiful, many of us fear we will lose our status, our value, and the love we need to survive. Perhaps that explains the number of women who've undergone cosmetic surgeries and now look like they've been standing in a wind tunnel! It's a desperate measure to counter what must feel like a desperate situation.

I've spent an enormous amount of energy over my lifetime trying to make things fit my mind's picture of how things *should* be, how others *should* be, how I *should* be. I tried to shape myself to fit the standards that the media fed me. I tried to control people and events in my life so that (I thought) I'd be happy. I spent *waaay* too much time and energy focused on my appearance and whether I was doing things "right." So much so that most of the time I felt like I was impersonating myself instead of just being myself.

I think your whole life shows in your face and you should be proud of that.
LAUREN BACALL

Character contributes to beauty. It fortifies a woman as her youth fades.
JACQUELINE BISSET

Looking back on my life, I notice that my efforts to be, look and act like I'm supposed to have not brought me ongoing joy and happiness. I'm talking down-deep happiness. How about you?

Pain is a great motivator, and I eventually figured out that trying to force people and circumstances to meet my picture of how I thought things should be didn't make me happy. Trying to live up to unattainable standards only frustrated me. It was actually quite exhausting and I paid dearly: depression, dissatisfaction, divorce, and eventually, chronic fatigue.

When my salon epiphany churned up years of influence that were embedded deep in my psyche, I wondered—*Why was I so concerned about what I looked like? Why was it so important to maintain the look of youth? What was the payoff? What was I so afraid of losing?*

Then it dawned on me—perhaps it was *power.*

Ka-ching!

Human beings are great negotiators. As females, we learn to use our looks and sexuality as bargaining chips, cashing them in to get what we want or need. We learn early on that we can hold great power over others, and we're not afraid to use it.

When you come right down to it, humankind isn't all that different from the animal kingdom. To attract a mate, animals engage in flashy displays of plumage and strength, perform elaborate rituals, and emit irresistible scents. For similar reasons, women paint their eyes, gloss their lips, spritz on perfume, don revealing clothing, and move in a seductive way that says, "Here I am, come get me—*if* I decide I want you." Men have their version of the dance as well, mostly focused on being big, strong and a good provider. This is heady stuff—both powerful and intoxicating—and there is nothing wrong with this behavior. It's hardwired!

But what happens when a woman moves beyond her reproductive years? Is she no longer desirable or valuable or important? Does losing the ability (or desire) to reproduce mean she loses her power?

Well, *yes…* depending on how you define power. Using your feminine wiles to get what you want may be easy and even feel good, but it is tenuous at best. Those who rely on it can suffer from low-level anxiety, knowing their power can fade or vanish at any time. This keeps us scanning the horizon for the next thing that will help us maintain a youthful image—the next fashion, makeup, diet, cosmetic procedure, etc. Sadly, constant vigilance means constant stress, which means adrenal depletion, which means we age quicker!

Stepping into her own authentic power, a woman of age learns to look carefully at the hand she's been dealt and ask herself what truly makes her *her*, rather then what makes her desirable to *others*.

Take a moment to list five characteristics that have nothing to do with your appearance but that make you uniquely *you*.

> Examples: *Great sense of humor, discerning intellect, ability to see the big picture, deep faith, compassionate heart, kindness, athletic ability, love of the outdoors, detail oriented, ability to sew, dance, sing, cook, listen, paint, write, etc.*

There is a different kind of power that comes from the wisdom of a lifetime of experience, rather than just dominance in the hierarchy.
BETTY FRIEDAN

_____   _____

_____   _____

_____   _____

By recognizing these attributes, it's easier to see that our true power comes from standing firm in our experience, our integrity, our heart and our unique character—and these do not vanish with age. In fact, they often grow. So why are so many of us insecure?

Is Something Wrong?

According to an MSNBC study on aging, Americans are living, on average, thirty years longer than we did a century ago. Because of the large number of people born during the baby-boom generation, those over age 55 will soon outnumber those under age 18 for the first time in history.[8]

Yet, if American culture were a car, surely the latest sexy, young, female pop icon would be driving it. Why? We are a culture bent on retaining our youth, committed to the belief that there is *something wrong* with the way things are—the way *we* are. We hang our hopes on the idea that somewhere out there is the solution to all that's wrong with us. We desperately hope that all we have to do to be happy is buy that shiny new object, or that new dress, or high-fashion shoes, or whatever Madison Avenue holds up as the "must have" fix of the month.

There is *something wrong* with being curvaceous, so we must diet and surgically alter ourselves to look like the models and movie stars. There is *something wrong* with showing panty lines under one's clothing, so we wear thong underwear. (I refuse to wear them. If you ask me, there is *something wrong* with having to make my bottom look smoothly attractive just so some person I don't even know can enjoy the view!) There is *something wrong* with getting and looking older, so we color our hair, endure plastic surgery, suck out the fat and inject chemicals into our character lines—all in an attempt to prove to society that we're still young and with it.

Even I don't wake up looking like Cindy Crawford.

SUPERMODEL
CINDY CRAWFORD

Too many of us take the *fashionistas'* point of view as the final word and discount our own sense of style and comfort. (One look at me and they would probably summon the panty-line police!) For a lifetime we have been encouraged to watch others for clues on how to dress, and to learn what's in and what's out. (Hence, our addiction to the celebrity culture.) Hemlines go up, hemlines come down. Jackets are boxy, jackets are tailored. Slacks are pencil thin, and then wide trouser legs are in. Skirts are everywhere, and just when you've invested a small fortune in them, they're out. We all want to fit in, but at what cost? The unspoken message is, "Spend your money, become part of the 'in' crowd, look like everyone else… and *then* you'll be accepted, loved and valued."

I've certainly done my share of conforming. I did my time as a servant to popular media—coloring my hair, altering my body, wearing the latest fashion and conforming to whichever standards might guarantee me a seat at the head table. But after so many years spent chasing someone else's standards, I was left empty. A voice echoed in my head, muttering, "Oh, *that* wasn't it. Maybe if I… (lose weight, get breast implants, buy a new outfit, color my hair, tan my skin), *then* I'll be okay." I wanted approval… no, I *needed* approval! And I was looking everywhere (except within) to find it. It was like being on a hamster wheel, chasing something I would never find.

Women who live for the next miracle cream do not realize that beauty comes from a secret happiness and equilibrium within themselves.

SOPHIA LOREN

Moving toward a Higher Intelligence

As I grew older and began to trust my instincts, it became easier to choose the things that were right for *me*. Through trial and error I learned to rely on my own sense of what works and what feels natural. Fashions and trends can be fun, and I'm not saying we should be walking

around in baggy brown potato sacks, chanting mantras
of acceptance and inner beauty. Choose styles and colors
that work for you and make you feel good. Who cares
if it's last year's color (and who says colors get different
years, anyway?). Wear shoes that support you in being an
active participant in life and that won't leave you crippled
with foot and back pain by the time you're 70. While it
can be fun to use fashion to express yourself—it's important to remember that your appearance does not define
who you are.

I'm still in the process of letting go of my *shoulds*. I'm
learning to accept that I am getting older and my hair
is naturally silver. Lines crisscross areas that used to be
smooth, and I will never see the likes of a flat belly again.
And I'm surviving. Better than that—I'm flourishing! I
finally understand that going gray does not mean… fade
to black.

Unfortunately, succumbing to the pressures of our
youth-and-beauty culture, many women are undergoing
cosmetic surgeries, believing it will change the way they
feel about themselves as they age. For some, it can be
an effective strategy to delay the inevitable. For others it
simply adds fuel to the fire of self-hate. Sadly, many of
us have seen women whose cosmetic surgery left them
looking nothing like their former selves. Along with the
sags and wrinkles, the expression and character have
also been erased from their face—rendering them rather
lifeless. There's always that risk.

If you believe cosmetically altering your aging face
or body will bring you the love and approval you seek, I
would suggest you dig a little deeper. After many cosmetic
alterations, the result is often a younger-looking version
of a woman who is still wondering, "Am I lovable? Am I
acceptable? Am I good enough?"

On this issue, I speak from experience. I learned earlier in life that altering my outsides provided only temporary relief from the pain and insecurity inside. When I was thirty-something, I too fell victim to this cultural pressure. I had breast augmentation surgery, for all the reasons I've described. I wanted to be desirable. I wanted to fit in. I wanted to be loved. I wanted big breasts!

Unfortunately, my personal demons—low self-esteem and lack of confidence—were augmented right along with my breasts. (They don't make breasts big enough to hide behind!) I felt unbalanced and out of kilter. I was uncomfortable with the glances and overt stares from men, because I felt inauthentic. I knew I was presenting a false image to the world. The attention focused on my breasts made me uneasy because *they* really weren't *me*. (There's a reason it's called *plastic* surgery.)

I never would have undergone the surgery if I hadn't believed that there was *something wrong* with me the way I was. Sadly, I actually thought larger breasts would make me more of the person I was supposed to be, thus making me more lovable. Enhanced breasts did not bring me more love, or joy, or contentment, or security. Today, being more comfortable with my sense of self, I would not choose surgery again.

I have no doubt there are women who love their plastic surgeries and simply don't or can't relate to this discussion. I am also aware that there are people with disfigurements or oversized breasts who benefit greatly from cosmetic surgery. The point to remember is that it's not *what* you do but *why* you do it. The reasons and intentions behind your decision are much more important than the decision itself.

More often than not, there is an underlying belief in *something wrong* that drives the need to alter oneself to meet an arbitrary standard of perfection. What many of us hope to accomplish through cosmetic procedures can only be achieved through careful examination of the beliefs we hold inside. Explore your beliefs and motives, love and accept yourself completely—then decide what (or if) to change. After all, if your body were for your eyes only, would you really choose to surgically alter it and endure all that pain and discomfort?

Perhaps it's our self-acceptance that needs the makeover.

Unfortunately, many women become so externally focused, so dependent on what others think and say about us, that we begin to lose touch with what we want for ourselves, making us easy targets for the marketers. Living in a world of "what's wrong" creates anger and frustration, burnout and disappointment, and fear about what the future holds.

When I stopped trying so hard to be someone else, it was so much easier to just be me. Remember, who you are does not change with surgery. It's just your *perception* of who you are that changes. You can save yourself a lot of money and pain by changing your perception of yourself—and forgoing the surgery.

Inside yourself or outside, you never have to change what you are, only the way you see it.
THADDEUS GOLAS

What's Really Wrong?

The *trouble actually lies with the rest of us* thinking that the advertising tactics aimed at the younger generation set the standards that all of us should live up to.

Many of us engage in an internal debate about whether or not to intervene and thwart the physical effects of aging. We've become so used to seeing perfect faces and bodies in the media, that we are often appalled when we look in the mirror and see the normal effects of aging: wrinkles, frown lines, gray hair and crepey skin. It doesn't jibe with our picture of what we're *supposed* to look like.

Living in the United States of Advertising, we are constantly bombarded with images of fashion, makeup and entertainment used to entice the young. In an effort to delay facing our own mortality, many of us adopt these standards as our own and think ourselves hip, young and with it. Somehow, we find ourselves trying to measure up to an airbrushed standard that doesn't even exist!

Each time we fall short of an expectation, it validates the belief that "there is something wrong with me." Slowly but surely, we are conditioned to believe we are defective. I would suggest that there is nothing wrong with us, but rather with the system that sets us up to appear defective.

Whether to intervene or not is a personal choice. While there are many non-invasive options available to smooth over the physical effects of aging, most of them are still beyond a budget of middle-class means. As I aged, I found it more useful to focus on an *attitude* of aging and less on the appearance of aging, although I have seen that one can definitely impact the other.

So, in a sense, I say *yes* to intervention. *Yes* to burning off the effects of negative perceptions. *Yes* to rendering immobile the beliefs that proclaim we are inadequate, too old, or that our life is over. *Yes* to an attitude-lift, not a face-lift. *No* to airbrushing our lives.

Perhaps some women under the age of 50 will have a difficult time relating to this message. I probably would have at that age. The cultural message to be "perfect" is louder than ever, and the younger generation could pay an even bigger price than we boomers are... unless we help them wake up to what's wrong with our culture. We seem to have crossed a line somewhere—and many women have abdicated their personal sense of self to be like the celebrities they see flaunted in their faces every day.

In the interest of our future generations, perhaps it's time Amazing Grays come forth and, reminiscent of the

There is no reality except the one contained within us. That is why so many people live such an unreal life. They take the images outside them for reality and never let the world within assert itself.
HERMANN HESSE

1960s, once again proclaim, "We won't take it anymore!" Haven't we had enough of trying to be perfect, enough of trying to meet an unattainable standard, enough of trying to look like the celebrities? (Who, by the way, have personal trainers, hairstylists, makeup artists, personal stylists and the money to purchase any procedure and product they desire.)

The real question is: *Are those who don't embody this standard of youth and beauty less valuable than those who do?* Aren't we all meant to have a shot at the best in life? Aren't we all deserving? Is there an age cutoff when we go from valued to discarded? How shallow have we become to attach such importance to one standard of beauty? Have we forgotten about the deeper, richer kinds of beauty? What about:

- The woman with the large nose and small eyes, whose kindness and generosity touch you deeply

- The short, stocky woman with the frizzy hair whose eyes sparkle with her power and presence

- The woman with the scarred face who makes you feel like the most important person in the room

We often walk away from these encounters saying to ourselves, "What a beautiful person!"

Ah, so there *is* another standard of beauty!

Perhaps there is a reason for all our different packaging. We each have a unique purpose to fulfill, and most would agree that our packaging is part of that journey. It seems inconceivable that our goal here on earth is for all of us to move toward the same standard of beauty, yet so many of us are willing to go under the knife to do just that. Keep in mind that our physicality is just a small piece of who we are—*and it's not even the piece we get to take with us when we leave this earth!*

If it truly was divine inspiration that put us all in different packages, then why are we trying to mess with Mother Nature?

Leading by example, and accepting our uniqueness at every stage of life, we Amazing Grays have an opportunity to influence an entire generation (or at least those willing to listen) to challenge our youth-and-beauty culture and accept the wisdom and freedom that comes with aging gracefully, knowing we are so much more than our physical bodies. By living our lives mindfully, authentically—with vitality and purpose—we can provide them with a roadmap to becoming Amazing Grays, too!

CHAPTER 4

The Key to Aging Gracefully

I FINALLY CAME TO UNDERSTAND that when it comes to growing older, I had only two choices: to accept or resist. This is the crossroads that every woman will eventually come to, and your choice will determine your quality of life, and ultimately affect your peace of mind, health, and depth of connection with others. It's a choice not to be taken lightly. I chose acceptance.

I'm not saying we should roll over and play dead. Far from it! Acceptance simply means to acknowledge *what is*: "Yes, I'm getting older. My days on this earth are numbered (which has always been true). My hair and body are losing some of the luster of youth. My face has wrinkles." None of those conditions are good or bad—they just *are*. It just *is* the way *it is*—and it has nothing to do with my value as a woman, unless I say so. I get to decide my experience of these conditions—putting my precious energy into the things I can and am willing do something about, and accepting those things I either cannot or am unwilling to change.

Grace: The outward expression of the inward harmony of the soul.
WILLIAM HAZLITT

43

This stage of life is an opportunity for a fresh start: a chance to reframe your life, redefine yourself, embrace your years of wisdom and experience, let go of the pieces that no longer serve you, and decide what you want to do next! It's time to make a conscious decision to move forward without keeping an eye on the rearview mirror.

I noticed that when I accepted and embraced my maturity, I felt vital, more authentic and excited about the possibilities that lay ahead. When I resisted the process and focused on trying to recover the look of my youth, I felt tired and depressed ('cause no matter how you try to erase them, the effects of time and gravity just keep showing up!). Instead of being the woman I am and living my life fully and authentically, I kept comparing myself to a standard that I'm not meant to live up to—and falling short. It was exhausting. Since I stopped trying to regain my youth, I actually *feel* more youthful. Go figure.

In her book *When You're Falling, Dive,* Cheri Huber writes: "When we accept responsibility for our lives, we make peace with all that is not as we would wish it to be. It's not that we gain the power to change circumstances, we develop the skill to determine our experience of those circumstances."[9]

And that's the key. When we accept responsibility for our *experience* of the aging process, we gain the freedom to redefine it.

Accepting something doesn't have to mean approval or agreement, resignation or defeat. Resignation pulls your head down, blinding you to possibilities. Acceptance allows you to hold your head up and look life in the eye, seeing something for what it is and simply acknowledging it as so, without passing judgment on its worth or validity. Once again, I noticed it was the *meaning* I attached to something—anything!—that determined how I experienced it.

Containing Resistance

Actually, I found acceptance was rather easy—it's *resisting* that's hard. Many of us spend more of our energy resisting life than we do living it! Resisting the aging process is like fighting life—and uses up valuable time and energy that could be better spent enjoying life.

Can you imagine what your life would look like if you could harness all the energy you use to resist life and simply *embrace* what is, knowing there is always enough of what you need and there truly is nothing wrong with you? It's a very different worldview than most of us hold... but what if?

Why do we resist? To maintain an outdated identity, to validate who we *think* we are. The pull of a culture of youth and beauty is powerful. Resistance is really the voice of our conditioning trying to say no to everything that doesn't support who it would like you to believe you are.

Suffering (being unhappy, dissatisfied, miserable, guilty, angry, worried, unfulfilled, distressed—you get the idea) is caused by wishing things were different than they are. You have this; you want that. This is happening; you want that to happen. You are here; you want to be there. You are 50; you want to be 30. Sound familiar? It's the opposite of acceptance!

When we dwell on what we wish were different, energy levels plummet. The unconscious mind mixes up a cocktail of sadness, pain, wistfulness, regret and guilt, and adds a splash of fear and disappointment to create the ultimate elixir of self-hate. We drink in the noxious mix and then stumble through life, trying to look happy. Who are we kidding? Our inner voices of self-loathing are exhausting! We are often left with a sense of anxiety that we're not doing what we're supposed to be doing.

Ours is a society of denial that conditions us to protect ourselves from any direct difficulty and discomfort. We expend enormous amounts of energy denying our insecurity, fighting pain, death, and loss, and hiding from the basic truths of the natural world and of our own nature.

JACK KORNFIELD

Sure, we can all find things to complain about. My own personal rantings tend to focus on the crumpling skin of my upper arms. I can take care of my arms by exercising and moisturizing them, but I can't undo past sun damage. Some days I just need to complain. How about you?

Rather than giving the voices of discontent free rein, we can contain our complaining. Give yourself five minutes a day to kvetch about your arms, your thighs, your tummy or anything else that bothers you. Let it all out—for five minutes! You can cover a lot of ground in that time. If there is more, save it for the next day. Then focus your remaining waking hours on the good news. You're *alive*, able to love, travel, work, sing, dance, spend time with family and friends, perhaps enjoy grandchildren, choose new experiences, express your creativity and learn new skills. It's just not useful to stay stuck in a complaining mode. Whatever you focus on expands!

Truthfully, if your sense of self disintegrates at the mere thought of looking older or going gray, perhaps it's time to take a closer look at how you define yourself and your worth as a woman.

If we focus on our defects and spend scads of time thinking about our flaws, what's wrong and the ways we don't measure up, we end up wasting precious time and energy—and drawing that reality to us! More importantly, nothing changes for the better, and we become caught in a cycle of berating ourselves for not measuring up. I can choose to hide my arms, feeling inadequate and defective, or I can (get a grip!) choose to accept that these are the arms I have now.

I have come to appreciate that these are the beautiful arms that allow me to embrace my precious grandbabies and all those I love. They reach out to help others, hug my hubby, and wave hello and goodbye. They allow me

Your suffering is the pain of holding onto that which no longer serves you.
KAHLIL GIBRAN

to write this book, carry my groceries, drive my car, open doors and do a thousand other things that would be difficult without them. In the face of this new understanding, doesn't it sound ridiculous to say, "I hate my arms (hips, thighs, belly, etc.)"?

Who set the standard that toned arms (or a flat stomach or smooth skin or skinny thighs) are what give a person value? Knowing that there is nothing wrong with me, I can lovingly embrace and accept who I am in the here and now. I watch the thoughts and fears about aging arise, and (most of the time) I just don't believe them.

I can hear some of you shouting, "I'm going to resist aging until I take my last breath! I'm going to color my hair, inject chemicals into my wrinkles, peel my skin, surgically lift my face and body and do whatever it takes to maintain the look of my youth!"

Okay. Breathe. I am not suggesting we stop taking care of ourselves, nor that we must all age in the same way. I like to be healthy and fit and put my best self forward as much as the next woman. We don't exist in some parallel universe once we cross the Big 5-0. We live in a society that clearly values appearance, and while I don't wish to be *defined* by how I look, I don't want to be defiled by it either. I have my hair styled in a way that is attractive yet easy to maintain. I wear clothing that is contemporary yet comfortable to me. I refuse to wear shoes that hurt. I exercise to remain fit so I can participate fully in life. I use moisturizer so my skin doesn't crack, and sometimes I even put on makeup!

It's just that now there seems to be a line I am unwilling to cross, stemming from a perspective on life that I would guess comes from living many decades. Through mindful self-examination, I have a deeper sense of what is truly important, where I want to spend my energy, and which issues and causes warrant my valuable time and attention. Do I want to continue to ingest or use toxic substances when I know they may shorten or debilitate my time here on earth? Do I want to spend large sums of money and time nipping and tucking when I believe there are more pressing needs in our world? Do I want to waste one more minute worrying about whether I look like the woman the media tells me I'm *supposed* to look like? For me the answer is finally—*no*. Others may make a different choice, and that's okay. That's the beauty of knowing your own mind. Youth may have its benefits, but the real gifts are unwrapped with the wisdom of age.

Practicing Acceptance

While it would be great to just decide to become more aware and accept life as it comes, it's not that easy when our conditioned voices have us convinced how hard it is. It takes consistent practice.

By practicing acceptance, it eventually becomes your response of choice. Before that develops, however, you can expect to bump up against a lot of resistance. As you move forward to accept *what is*, your inner voices will torment you with any number of nasty retorts. Perhaps these sound familiar:

I have gray hair.
> *Oh no! You better color it or you'll look old and unattractive. Who wants to hang around with an old lady?*

My face is becoming wrinkled.
> *Quick—get to a surgeon or people will think you don't care about yourself! You will never measure up, but you'd better keep trying.*

My thighs look dimpled.

Oh gawd. Cover them up. Go buy a cellulite cream to rid yourself of this blight. See, if you ate better and exercised more, you wouldn't look like this now. Shame on you.

I'm carrying a few extra pounds.

Get to the gym—now! You eat like a pig and have no self-control. You can never follow through on a diet. This is what you deserve!

Whew. No acceptance there! The voice of your conditioning is definitely *not* your friend.

When I obsess about all the things I perceive are wrong with my body and my life, these thoughts become the center of my attention, occupy the majority of my time, and most importantly, color my experience. There's not a lot of room for anything else. I find peace only when I refuse to believe the cacophony of voices in my head, confirming how defective I am, how I don't measure up.

Eventually, by paying attention, I came to realize that the quality and tenor of my thoughts greatly influenced my sense of well-being and energy levels. My experience has shown me that when I focus on "what's wrong" I feel heavy, depressed and tired. When I am turning toward or engaging in those things or activities I enjoy, I feel light, joyful and energized, free from the voices of my conditioning. Have you found that to be true for you? I've learned that if I get out of my own way and surrender, life will live me. That's a scary thought to a lot of us. It feels like giving up control of your life, like the old "blowing in the wind" mentality. Our inner voices would like us to believe that so we can stay "safe" by remaining under their influence. Don't buy it. Acceptance can be very freeing.

When you eventually see through the veils to how things really are, you will keep saying again and again, "This is certainly not like we thought it was."
JALALUDDIN RUMI

Accepting Your Beauty

Our aging bodies provide us ample opportunity to practice acceptance. (Especially after 50!) As women, we have learned to be critical of our bodies as we compare them to an unattainable standard. However, as we age and integrate new levels of awareness with a discerning intellect, we begin to challenge the prevailing standards and eventually accept that we are not defective. Not only are we not defective, we are beautiful in our own right. We just need to claim it.

Enjoy your body. Use it every way you can. Don't be afraid of it or of what other people think of it. It's the greatest instrument you'll ever own.

KURT VONNEGUT

How do we do that?

~ Take a moment and draw a basic front, back and side profile of your body (three separate drawings).

~ Draw an arrow to the parts you *dislike* and jot down what's wrong with them.

~ Now label the parts you especially *like*. What do you like about them? Why?

~ Do you have more likes than dislikes? Or vice versa?

~ What benchmark are you using to measure against?

~ What do your inner voices say to you when you don't measure up to those benchmarks?

~ Choose one body part that you currently judge as inadequate. How do you know it is inadequate? Who told you?

~ Imagine your daughter or best friend complaining about that part of their body. What would you say to them? Can you accept that advice for yourself?

~ Make a conscious choice to lovingly accept and embrace all parts of you, one by precious one.

It's only by accepting what *is* that we can take steps to change how we feel. Indulging in an inner dialogue that hates and berates parts of you actually reinforces an unhappy reality and makes you feel older. In your mind's eye, a flaw becomes who you are, i.e., a person who will forever have big hips, fat thighs, a poochy belly, or whatever your particular demon is. Your conditioning creates unhappiness and suffering by affirming that there is something wrong with you and is constantly yearning for things to be different than they are. Once again we are reminded that whatever you focus on, positive or negative, ultimately determines your experience.

Accepting what *is* doesn't mean that your thighs will be instantly slim, or your tummy will be flat, or your crow's feet will disappear. It simply means that rather than believing that you have unworthy or unattractive parts, you can choose to respond differently. Rather than feeling inadequate and full of loathing, you can choose to love who you really are in all your magnificence. As you learn to love and accept yourself, your ability to extend love and acceptance to others also expands.

Through my various practices, I have finally come to understand that the non-stop commentary in my head is not *me*. Those persistent voices of discontent proclaiming that there is *not enough* and that there is *something wrong* are not telling the truth. This is Big. Understanding that I am so much more than the rambling conversation in my head has opened me up to experience life as it was meant to be lived—as it *really* was meant be lived—moment by moment.

Rather than responding to the pressures of our inner chatter, I'm suggesting we accept a new authority: our own authentic nature, that conscious, compassionate core of our being that, when we slow down and pay attention, will guide us into choosing options that are in our best

For fast-acting relief, try slowing down.
LILY TOMLIN

interest, our highest good. By reminding ourselves that we are not our personality, our body or our emotions, we regain the inner knowing of who we *really* are.

Peace comes from living in full and total acceptance of what is, with no longing, no shoulding, no fear, no struggle. To be at peace means to be *in* acceptance—no resistance, no need to make things different than they are.

Embracing this point of view is the very definition of what it means to create a new beginning.

∞

For attractive lips, speak words of kindness.
For lovely eyes, seek out the good in people.
For a slim figure, share your food with the hungry.
For beautiful hair,
let a child run their fingers through it once a day.
For poise, walk with the knowledge that you never walk alone.
People, even more than things, have to be restored, renewed,
revived, reclaimed and redeemed; never throw out anyone.
AUDREY HEPBURN

CHAPTER 5

Shift Happens (When You Choose It)

OMEONE ONCE SAID THAT the only person who really likes change is a wet baby. I agree! While I am choosing to age gracefully, I've certainly done my share of kicking and screaming along the way. Many of us struggle with the social ramifications of what it means to grow older. Didn't you throw away that AARP membership application the first time you received it? *"No, this can't be for me!"* Surprise, surprise.

Realizing (um, having it shoved in our faces—thank you very much, AARP) that we are now the senior generation (or just a small step away) can be unnerving. We finally get that we don't have forever. The things that previously defined us are changing, and we begin to experience a slow unraveling of the fabric that is our life. We can work feverishly trying to mend it, or we can gracefully gather up the loose threads and weave them into a tapestry of possibilities.

As I struggled with my aging body and my changing roles, I discovered that I wasn't a very good weaver! There were way too many pulled threads and frayed edges.

Slowly, I began to realize I needed to make a monumental identity shift, detaching from the things that had previously defined my life. By tapping into the deep well of wisdom within and mindfully staying open to possibilities, I realized that I didn't need to work at becoming someone; I already was someone.

I learned that to age gracefully I needed to accept responsibility for my experience of aging, teach others how to treat me, challenge my negative inner chatter and fully engage with the activities, people and events that bring a smile to my lips. I came to understand that when I defined myself primarily through my physical body, I became disheartened as things started to loosen up and succumb to gravity. Sure, my looks matter—but they are not who I am! By living mindfully and reaffirming that my physical self is simply part of a greater whole, I am able to appreciate that I am on this earth for a reason, and I still have much to offer. Gradually, I was able to give myself back to myself.

Ultimately, to deny my age is to disrespect myself, my life experience, and my hard-earned wisdom. Owning the reality that I am now part of a generation of Amazing Grays was a powerful wake-up call to continue living my life consciously, in the here and now, savoring every moment. Yes, all the talk about coming face-to-face with one's mortality as you age is true—but it's a good thing! I was motivated to take stock of my life, let go of the activities, things and people that keep me stuck in the past or no longer bring me joy, and remain open to what life has in store for me.

I found that hanging on to what was only created exhaustion. Wishing life was different is to deny the truth of what is. Eventually, to find peace, we must embrace our changing bodies and roles, and simply enjoy the view from where we are.

Age is an issue of mind over matter. If you don't mind, it doesn't matter.
MARK TWAIN

Wisdom doesn't necessarily come with age. Sometimes age just shows up all by itself.
TOM WILSON

And, I can tell you… the view is magnificent, *depending on who's doing the looking!* Looking through the eyes of my conditioning, all my fears and beliefs about what it means to be old come to the surface. Frail, sick, tired, weak, stuck in our ways, housebound, fragile, forgetful, rambling—yuck! This will be my experience *only* if I choose to ignore my options and believe the picture that was programmed into me. Looking through the eyes of my authentic, conscious, compassionate self, I see a very different picture. It's a matter of choice. Perhaps the best facelift we can all hope for is a knowing smile of acceptance!

Good Grief

Sometimes it can be difficult to age with grace when it feels like so much is being lost to the sands of time.

Some of us are losing dear friends and family to the ravages of disease. While the pain of watching a loved one slip away can be excruciating, being present for their transition can be a gift—to all involved. Once again, it's all in how you frame it. It can be another opportunity to embrace the preciousness of life and, once you have grieved, a chance to allow your loved one to live on in your memory.

Most life transitions trigger a grieving process. In addition to the pain of losing loved ones, many of the changes that come with aging are also perceived as losses: we lose our reproductive status, our girlish figures, our smooth skin, our flat bellies, and yes, our hair color. It doesn't seem right!

With each letting go, there is a new beginning. Hanging on to what was keeps us from experiencing what is. I found that in order to embrace the new, I needed to

Life is expressed in a perpetual sequence of changes. The birth of a child is the death of the baby, just as the birth of the adolescent is the death of the child.

ARNAUD DESJARDINS

grieve and let go of the old. Straddling the chasm between the two, I was faced with more questions than answers:

Who am I becoming? What is my purpose now? What role am I going to play?

I suspect questions of this nature arise anytime we encounter one of life's many milestones. For women, many of these turning points are sparked by physical changes, which often stir up an emotional soup.

Having a hysterectomy is a huge transition for many women and often triggers deep grief. I remember feeling a profound sadness after my operation, sobbing inconsolably for hours. I was barely 40. My grief was not so much triggered by a sudden drop in hormones (my ovaries remained), but by the stark realization that I was no longer a fertile woman. There was finality to that, something that touched me more deeply than I ever expected. It was as if who I was changed in an instant, and the social position of women in their reproductive years was no longer mine. I was surprised to realize how much of my identity was invested in my fertility! I grieved the loss of my young, lustful, fertile self and was unsure of what was to come. Years later, I found myself immersed in a similar feeling and cried for weeks when my only daughter left for college. Now, as I face the passage into maturity, I am touched once again by a profound sadness. Not only is my place in the fabric of life changing, but loved ones are crossing over. How do we navigate the grief and uncertainty of such significant transitions?

Rather than tune out and ignore the lightning and thunder within, I made the decision to turn and face it.

In our own time and in our own order, most of us experience the various stages of grief: denial, anger, bargaining, depression and acceptance.[10] Actually, these were originally called the five stages of receiving catastrophic news, which is often how many of us view the realization that we are over 50! Many of us *deny* that we're now seniors, experience *anger* that we got old (this wasn't supposed to happen!), *bargain* with the plastic surgeons, get *depressed* that in spite of all our efforts we're still getting older and finally, if we're wise, *accept* that we still have the gift of life and can choose to age gracefully.

By accepting that change is part of life's rich tapestry, I gave myself permission to grieve the losses that come with age. It's important work. Any loss, perceived or real, must be acknowledged. Cry, observe, vent, journal, meditate, pray, talk to a friend or therapist—but don't ignore it. When we hold these feelings inside, we become depressed, unmotivated and cranky (to put it nicely). Often, by simply noticing them, naming them, and giving them the space to exist, the feelings express themselves and soon the intensity diminishes on its own. In order to live in the *now* we must let go of the past.

What are some of the "losses" you anticipate or have experienced as you approach midlife? Are there leftover pockets of grief that still yearn for expression?

~ Make a list.

_____

_____

_____

_____

~ Are they real losses (loss of smooth skin, loss of a loved one) or something conjured up by a fear (loss of desirability)?

~ How do you grieve these losses?

~ What helps you through your grief?

~ Who will you be without these people or things in your life?

~ What might you learn or gain?

~ Can you use these answers to bring more compassion to the parts of you that are hurting?

Contemplating these questions, resolving these lifelong issues and grieving them fully is making us ready for whatever comes next. Our bodies guide us in clearing out the old, helping us untie the emotional knots of our past in order to make room for a new experience of life. It's as if we are no longer allowed to let the past hold our minds and bodies hostage. Our eyes are given the ability to see the bigger picture, and we open our hearts to receive it.

Letting Go

Some losses are very tangible. Thousands of boomers are losing their parents and are coming to grips with the fact that they are now without the safety net of parental love, support and guidance. The buffer is gone. Some feel orphaned.

For many of us, our parents were our unabashed champions, the people whom we could count on to be there for us (in spite of the misunderstandings and dysfunction between us). They were a shoulder to cry on, a reality check, and a place to lay our head. Losing a parent can suddenly make us feel like that scared-out-of-our-mind kid on the high-dive once again, but this time there is no one there to catch us when we jump.

Not all of us had a close relationship with our parent(s), but regardless of the quality of that connection, they were once our precious mommy or daddy. The child in us who took refuge in that relationship is left facing a deep hole. The grief of losing a parent ranks right up there with losing a child or spouse. It must be honored, no matter how old you are when it occurs.

This sense of loss is also felt when a parent becomes infirm and childlike. Alzheimer's, Parkinson's, dementia and other debilitating diseases rob us of their essence, leaving us with difficult and demanding responsibilities and emotions, taxing both our patience and resources. We find ourselves grieving the loss of someone who still lives, and that can be confusing.

I once asked a nurse how she dealt with her ornery and difficult patients, and her answer was deeply moving: "I remind myself that they were once somebody's baby." Recognizing their innocence helps us tap into our compassion. Appreciating our ailing parents for who they were and dealing with them as they are is often the best we can hope for.

If your parents become more demanding or dependent, ask for help and be sure to take care of the parts of you that are hurting. The voices in your head may be loud and abusive. They may insist you should do more, but do not take on more than you can handle. Remember, those internal voices only reflect your conditioning. Ignore them and continue to do the best you can.

When I lost my father, I noticed that while I mourned the immediate loss of his life, the grief passed rather quickly. I later came to understand that, having already made my peace with our history over the years, I was not left holding a huge bag of pain and regret. Ultimately, I did not need to mourn the loss of the *opportunity* to heal.

Grieving without regrets can make it much easier to process your pain. If possible, take time to make peace with that relationship while your parents are still living. It may require introspection, emotional honesty, and forgiveness. Oftentimes, it involves accepting that they will never become the parent you wanted or needed them to be. Your younger self grieves this. You do not necessarily have to involve your parent(s) in a dialogue to make peace with the past—this is about *you*, not them. Employ the services of a good therapist or clergy person if you need guidance through this process.

If your parents are already gone, you can create the opportunity to forgive them and express your feelings through journaling or talking to someone who can be a tender-hearted witness for you. There are also grief recovery groups that can provide you with sanctuary and put you in the company of others who are facing similar losses.

Sometimes, when you are ready, it's helpful to write about your memories, view family videos, and go through old photographs. Looking back and seeing the family in joyful times, celebrating life's milestones, can be a comforting connection to the cycle of life.

Losing your parents can be a profound reminder of your own mortality, but when they pass, it's important to remember that *we* are still alive. Someday it will be our children and grandchildren who will mourn our passing—but we're not gone yet! Don't waste another minute on petty grievances. Focus on creating a strong bond with your family and friends, letting them know how loved and cherished they are. Spend time together making memories. The grandchildren will soon forget about that new toy you gave them, but they will always remember spending time with you telling silly jokes, going to the park, and coloring away lazy afternoons.

If your parents are still with you, take the opportunity to create an audio or video of them talking about their lives, their regrets, their loves and losses. What kernels of wisdom about life might they want to leave you or their grandchildren? While we often think to leave a will to deal with the disposition of our *valuables*, most of us haven't given much thought to how we might pass on our *values*. Creating what has become known as an "ethical will" can be a lasting gift for generations to come. (Visit *www. ethicalwill.com* for guidelines.)

Perhaps one of the greatest respects we can pay our parents is to live a life that is deeply rewarding and full of love. By doing so, we fulfill every parent's deepest wish for their child: to be happy. What a treasured legacy to leave for future generations!

What legacy would you like to leave?

~ If a child turned to you for guidance, what would you tell them about this journey through life? What nuggets of wisdom would you like them to tuck into their pockets to draw strength from as they follow their own path?

~ Take a moment and write down three kernels of wisdom that you might impart to a child— perhaps your own grandchild. What have you learned along the way that might help guide them on their life journey?

1. _____

2. _____

3. _____

~ Use these nuggets of wisdom as your own touch-stone to remind yourself about what's really important in life. Respect your journey and the wisdom you have garnered along the way. Be willing to share it with others—and be sure to walk your talk!

If you don't live it, it won't come out your horn.
CHARLIE PARKER

Becoming a Wise-Woman

As I matured, I began to look differently at the things that had given my life value for so many years. My nurturing gene has somehow switched to neutral, and I sometimes resent the household demands on my time. I'm no longer looking for my other half, finally accepting that I am whole unto myself. I'm no longer searching for security and fulfillment in the material world. I'm moved to find ways to make a difference beyond my immediate family. I'm no longer consumed with my appearance; I just want an easy hairstyle and minimal upkeep. I know the difference between quantity and quality. Despite my own creature comforts and career success, I know it's neither the things I possess nor my achievements that bring about the deepest sense of inner peace and fulfillment. Perhaps you have had similar realizations?

If we look to our future with fearful eyes, we struggle with an underlying resistance to this next stage of life—infertile of body, but glorious with spirit. As women, we move through the seasons of our lives intrinsically knowing it is not a linear process. We spiral through various aspects of each phase until we gradually ready ourselves for the next.

Ultimately we reach menopause, and if we choose to age consciously, we mature into our wise-woman (oh my goodness, no!) crone years. While the term has often been vilified in modern times, a crone was once recognized and appreciated for her wisdom, knowledge and spiritual maturity. Crone typically meant "wise one" and "revered elder of the circle." That's a good thing!

Menopause is defined as the pause of the menses. The blood of life no longer flows out of a woman but is held inside to help her give birth to her own inner wisdom, spirituality and knowing. At this point a woman can stitch together a lifetime of experience and wisdom into a cloak of empowerment, or she can live small, bemoan the process, and envy and emulate the younger generation.

Becoming a wise-woman crone is not an automatic bestowal of honor, based solely on the number of years one has existed on the planet. Not every woman in her post-menopausal years has earned this position. It comes from assimilating one's life experience and lessons learned into an integrated philosophy of wisdom; from fully embracing the sacred journey we are all on; and from healing the parts of ourselves that have been wounded. It is a title for a woman who uses her gifts of wisdom to become a spiritual midwife of sorts to the younger genera-tion or the world community at large. I would consider it an honor to be looked upon as a wise-woman crone.

Unfortunately, just hearing the word "crone" stirs up feelings of foreboding for many women. In fairy tales, the crone is depicted as an old, withered, humpbacked witch with a hooked nose who just might eat little children. When she appears, you know something bad is going to happen, often a death. This image is imprinted in our earliest years, and it's easy to see why many of us recoil at the notion of becoming a crone. Seeing the crone as a harbinger of death brings our unresolved fears about dying to the surface.

Truthfully, it just might be the fear of dying that keeps most of us resisting the aging process. Fear of dying is often the unspoken regret of not living life to its fullest potential. As we get older and begin to rub shoulders with our mortality, some of us wonder… *Have I done every-thing I came to do? Have I wasted my precious time? Have I made a difference?*

There is nothing any of us can do about what did or did not happen in the past. Beating yourself up about it is a waste of the time you have *now*. Every moment you spend in fear or regret marks a little death—the death of a moment (the one you lost to fear or regret). Lest we forget, all of life is interconnected and there are no disposable moments.

Many of us are so busy running in place, accruing stuff and assuring we look good that we become detached from the natural cycle of things. Let's face it: everything eventually dies. We just don't know when. Fearing death or ignoring it will not change that fact. Neither will trying to look younger. Do we really think that if we fool others into believing we are younger than we truly are, maybe Mother Nature will believe it too?

You can't fool Mother Nature!

The most effective antidote I have found is to face my issues about dying head-on and know that these fears are manufactured and kept alive by the voices of my lifelong conditioning. By acknowledging these fears without *believing* them, I can move on with the business of living fully in the moment, which is where life resides.

Rather than preoccupy your mind with the fear of death, define how you want to *live* life from here on out. Choose the activities and people that support you in living purposefully. Being present for your life now will allow you to experience it fully, day by day, so that when the final curtain does fall, you can let go with a deep bow and a knowing smile of satisfaction.

Can you imagine your own memorial service?

~ Imagine you are attending your own funeral; of course, no one can see you. Where is it being held? What music is playing? Are there flowers? What kind? Who is attending?

~ Imagine each person who is important to you standing up to speak, one at a time. What would

Daring to live means daring to die at any moment but also means daring to be born, crossing great stages of life in which the person we have been dies, and is replaced by another with a renewed vision of the world, and at the same time realizing that there will be many obstacles to overcome before we reach the final stage of enlightenment.

ARNAUD DESJARDINS

you like to hear them say about you and how you lived your life?

~ Are there any changes you need to make now to ensure you leave the legacy you want?

The legacy we leave

A wise-woman knows that she creates her own experience by the thoughts she projects onto the world around her and the actions she takes to support them. She no longer defines herself by listening to the toxic voices within. She orders up a life that reflects her enthusiasm and keeps her young at heart. She is rooted in her spirituality, knowing she is so much more than her physical body. She trusts her inner wisdom to guide her in making choices that embody the best of her talents and abilities. She is able to fully grieve the past, making room for the present. She is comfortable in her own skin, no longer needing to emulate her younger self. She fully inhabits her body—wrinkles, poochy tummy, crepey neck and all!

Accepting our new role as wise-women, we can share our newfound authentic sense of self with the next generation of aspiring wise-women. Just as we have been both enriched and challenged by our mothers' generation—as Amazing Grays, we have an opportunity to leave a legacy of self-love, acceptance and authenticity to the culture of women following in our footsteps.

Beautiful young people are accidents of nature, but beautiful old people are works of art.
ELEANOR ROOSEVELT

Becoming a Grandparent

As many of us have discovered, the most fun is becoming a wise-woman grandparent! The average age of a new grandmother is just 47.[11] By this age, while men are making their way through a midlife crisis, many women are just starting their midlife quest. Many of us are going back to school, starting new careers, creating businesses of our own and traveling the world. We're picking up the creative pursuits we neglected for so many years, and engaging our energy in all sorts of new adventures. For many of us, grandparenting is a natural—and eagerly anticipated—new adventure.

I had no idea it would be so profound! I was moved to tears when I heard my daughter sing lullabies to her new little bundle. Looking into that sweet baby's eyes, I was overcome with the awe of seeing her future and my past in the present moment.

When my misty eyes cleared, I finally got to wondering: What does it mean to be a grandma today? In my mind, the word "grandma" belonged to the soft, wrinkly woman who had loved me so well and was always encouraging me to eat more. Memories of a round, red-cheeked woman in the kitchen did not mesh with my identity as a vibrant, empowered woman of the world. After all, today's grandma is more likely to be at the gym with her iPod or on the computer counting up her frequent flyer miles for a trip to Costa Rica. So when I first heard the word "grandma"—applied to *me*!—I recoiled. What did you call me?

Once I recovered, I knew I needed to redefine that role for myself. The first step was to figure out what I wanted my grandchildren to call me. Trying on a few names to see how they felt, I finally settled on "Nonni." It resonated, was easy to pronounce, and most impor-tantly, I had no preconceived notions attached to the word. My granddaughter's paternal grandmother chose to be called "Amachi," stemming from her Basque heritage. Other women have proudly become Nana, Lola, Giggi, Grammy, Granny, Mutti, Meme and Oma—and a number of amusing versions that come with a child's mispronunciation!

When I became a Nonni, I was in the throes of menopause. My emotions were raw and sweet—and bordering on emotional incontinence! I cried each time I had to leave my granddaughter, as they lived four hours away. I was saddened by the distance between us and my inability to participate in her everyday life. I harbored fantasies of just dropping by, of taking her to the park and out for ice cream on hot summer days. Moving closer was not an option, and I carried a deep sadness that this part of my life didn't look like I had dreamed it to be.

Then I had the proverbial a-ha! I realized that I was causing myself great suffering by wishing things were different. It was easy to point to all the reasons why I should be unhappy, but in the end, I had a choice: I could be miserable about the situation, or I could accept that they live far away and be happy that I have them in my life at all! Either way, they still live far away. All my kvetching and wishing it were different was not helping, nor could it change the reality of the situation. This was simply another opportunity to accept what is.

To make peace within, I looked at what I *could* do. I made a commitment to go see them every four to six weeks and to have them to my home for a week during the summer months. Add in the occasional long weekend and most holidays, and we've been able to create a very fulfilling relationship despite the distance.

Being with small children is a joyous spiritual practice. I make sure that when I am with them, I am really *with* them. I put my work on the back burner and focus on being completely present. Then, we do their work! We play, read books, take walks, color, paint, swim, run like silly banshees through the sprinklers, and go visit the monkeys at the zoo. It's the perfect chance to practice one of the many gifts of maturity—knowing *now* is all there is.

Building and maintaining a strong bond with your grandchildren is a group project. Talk it through with their parents and let them know what kind of relationship you'd like to create with your grandchildren. How much time would you like to spend with them? Do you want to be their babysitter, or most definitely not? Some of us chafe at the idea of being built-in babysitters or raising our offsprings' children. Some of us delight in the possibility. There is no right or wrong way to do it, as long as you all work together to figure out what is in the best interests of everyone—*especially* the little ones.

The key to a satisfying experience is to be aware that we all have expectations about what grandparenting should look like. These "shoulds" come from our role models, family beliefs, and society's depictions of what a grandma is—and these conditioned expectations will compromise your peace of mind. It might feel wrong to say, "I've raised mine, now you raise yours." But if you want to be free to pursue your own interests, travel the world, and dance the night away, there is nothing wrong with that. It's just important to communicate your wishes in a loving manner, and stick to your guns.

If you don't have grandchildren of your own, there are many youngsters out there who would love to have a grandma. Go find them. Remember, you're an amazing woman—you create your own experience.

Simple Choices

What are our options? We know how to be healthy— eat a balanced diet, exercise, don't smoke, maintain a positive attitude, and stay present and engaged with life. Order up the picture of your life that supports *you* in staying active, engaged and happy. Take steps that will ensure the quality of life that you desire. That's not to say there won't be challenges. We just deal with them in the moment they occur, acknowledging the issue and accepting what *is*, remembering once again that worrying about what might happen is simply suffering in advance. Many of us will experience health challenges, some inherited, some earned, but these issues need not define us. Are you going to be a person limited by arthritis, or a joyful, engaged, active participant in life who also happens to have arthritis?

From a centered place, it is possible to age gracefully, enthusiastically, joyfully. It's not easy, but it is simple. Choosing to view life through the eyes of compassionate awareness, I see that there is no such thing as the future. There is only now, now, now—moment after moment. By living each one fully, caring for myself and others in each moment, and engaging mindfully with the life in front of me, I can age with joy, grace and gratitude.

And so can you.

PART TWO

PHYSICAL
PERSPECTIVES

Becoming
Body Wise

Life is not a journey to the grave with the intention of
arriving safely in a pretty and well preserved body,
but rather to skid in broadside,
thoroughly used up,
totally worn out,
and loudly proclaiming—
WOW—What A Ride!

UNKNOWN

Becoming Body Wise

ONE OF THE MOST PRECIOUS RESOURCES we have been gifted is a body. Unfortunately, as we move past our 40s and slip into the tumultuous waters of menopause, some days we'd rather leave it behind! Between sweaty nights, changing shapes, unpredictable hormones, and graying hair, an aging body can feel like someone else's! We wonder:

Why is there so much more of me? What happened to my desire? Does my partner still find me desirable? Why is sex sometimes painful? How can I control my hot flashes without putting my health at risk? Are hair dyes safe? How does one go from dyed to natural hair? Will I be attractive with silver hair? I have another question... but I can't remember what it is!

How do you navigate the changes, the uncertainty, and the hot flashes without losing your mind? By embracing the experience and listening closely for the messages.

As we cycle through the seasons of life, Mother Nature's wisdom provides many wake-up calls to help facilitate our personal journey. Our physical body is always communicating with us. Unfortunately, many of us just aren't paying attention. By quieting our inner chatter, we can begin to listen to our wise body.

Much as we'd like to believe we are in control, nature has the upper hand. When we look in the mirror and see a rounder body with a wrinkled face and graying hair... it's time to laugh! Not a chuckle, not a belly laugh, but an all-out body laugh! Flood your body with "feel good" energy and stop taking yourself so seriously!

By responding to these changes with humor and insight, we can appreciate how fortunate we are to have gotten this far.

CHAPTER 6

How Do We Age?

H AVE YOU BEEN SHOCKED by your aging body? Have you noticed that the condition of the body you always took for granted seemed to change… overnight? My body continues to surprise me. The skin above my knees is beginning to take on the folds of a Shar-Pei puppy, my forearms crinkle when I push my sleeves up, and I carry my own personal flotation device wherever I go. What's with that? How does this happen? What makes our bodies age? I needed to know.

From my research, I learned that we age in two ways: genetically and metabolically. The first we can do little about; the second we have a great deal of control over.

Every strand of DNA in your body is capped on both ends, like the plastic ends of a shoelace, with something called a *telomere*. Likened to the leader tape at either end of an audiocassette, telomeres protect our genetic data. Each time a cell divides, the telomere is shortened. We cannot lengthen them or stop them from shortening. Over time, the ends become "frayed" and the cell receives a message to stop replicating. This process is called "aging." Telomeres alone do not determine how long we live, but they are a key component.

Another key factor in aging is the formation of *free radicals*, toxic molecules that can lead to *oxidative stress*. These free radicals (isn't that what they called many of us in the 1960s?) attack our cells, tissues, arteries and DNA. Some come from the environment (sunlight, pollution), and some are consumed (smoking, alcohol, and poor nutrition). Left unchecked, these oxidants ravage our bodies and can lead to cardiovascular disease and related ailments.

A third important factor in aging is *glycation*. Glucose (sugar) from the foods we eat binds to things it has no business binding to—DNA, proteins and fats—rendering them unable to do their jobs. Among other things, this compromises the collagen in our arteries and they eventually lose their elasticity and become rigid.

I learned that stress plays a big role in shortening telomeres and increasing free radicals, so it makes sense that learning to let go of the small stuff and incorporating some form of stress reduction (prayer, meditation, exercise, yoga) into your everyday life can actually help you live longer.

The first wealth is health.

RALPH WALDO EMERSON

Taking excellent care of our body is a wise, but not always easy, choice. We are inundated with information about healthy aging: stop smoking, limit alcohol consumption, eat more healthfully and exercise regularly. Hearing these recommendations over and over, it's easy to ignore them. "Oh yeah, I'll start that next week. Oh yeah, I'll do that tomorrow. Oh yeah, I do need to start exercising more." And suddenly, you're 50! 55! 60! Then you hear yourself saying, "Oh yeah, my cholesterol is high. Oh yeah, I don't have the energy I used to have. Oh yeah, my skin looks like leather." Oh NO! When it comes right down to it, we are products of the choices we make (and remember, doing nothing is also a choice). Ultimately, aside from inherited conditions and accidents, we all have the face, body and physical health we earn.

The health gurus suggest we drink lots of pure water (half your body weight in ounces per day) and choose organic foods whenever we can. (Pesticides collect in your body over time.) Eat fresh, colorful fruits and vegetables that are rich in antioxidants (vitamins A, C and E, CoQ10, alpha lipoic acid, selenium and cartenoids) to help combat free radicals and help prevent cancer, stroke and heart disease. Minimize the "white" foods: processed flour, sugar, potatoes, and rice. They suggest we take a daily antioxidant and a multi-vitamin and mineral supplement, and minimize our exposure to unhealthy factors such as cigarette smoke and junk food.

Those who think they have no time for bodily exercise will sooner or later have to find time for illness.
EDWARD STANLEY

And last but certainly not least, we're told to keep our weight down and exercise. For good reason! Exercise reduces stress, lowers blood pressure, lowers bad choles- terol, raises good cholesterol, fights osteoporosis, induces weight loss, improves bowel regularity, is a natural and non-addictive sleep aid, lowers blood sugar, reduces joint stiffness and is a mild antidepressant! "But I don't like to exercise" doesn't fly anymore—even moderate activity pays big dividends. According to Dr. Harvey Simon in *The No-Sweat Exercise Plan:*

- 55 flights of stairs a week results in a 33 percent lower death rate.

- 1 hour of gardening a week equates to a 66 percent lower risk of sudden heart attack.

- Walking one hour a week (10 minutes a day!) lowers the risk of coronary artery disease by 51 percent.

- Exercising for 30 minutes twice a week results in a 43 percent lower mortality risk.[12]

If it weren't for the fact that the TV set and the refrigerator are so far apart, some of us wouldn't get any exercise at all.
JOEY ADAMS

In his book *Younger Next Year for Women,* Henry Lodge writes, "When you don't exercise, your muscles let out a steady trickle of chemicals that tell every cell to decay, day after day after day."[13] Is that the message you want to be sending your body? We are built to move. Every cell in your body (except for your brain) is constantly being replaced with new cells. The health of those new cells will be determined by the quality of attention you give your body—through exercise, diet and state of mind.

Notice what your inner voices are saying to you after reading this. Are they beating you up for not exercising? Giving you reasons why you just *can't* exercise? Suggesting you don't have the time or energy? Here's an opportunity to make a fresh start. You can believe the voices, or you can brush them off and make a plan to get out and walk, dance, skip or jump your way into fitness. Call a friend for support.

First You Hear a Whisper

Without good health, our life stalls as we turn our time, attention and resources to resuscitating it. Good health is more than eating well, exercising and going in for regular check-ups. It's about the attitude with which we embrace life. It's about accepting responsibility for our choices.

As human beings, we become so entrenched in our habits that we often just keep doing what we've always done. We disregard the signals of discontent, drive our bodies mercilessly, and ignore the road signs. It's not until you stop long enough to pay attention that you will hear the whisperings (or rumblings) from within.

At first, the message comes as a gentle whisper. If you don't respond, there might be a (metaphorical) poke in the ribs. If you still won't listen, you just might fall, scrape your knees and bleed, and if that doesn't get your attention, you might experience a major trauma, perhaps an illness or accident.

Many women who have been through a major trauma or health crisis talk about an intuitive whisper they ignored, one that told them to change course. They felt the prod in the ribs but rationalized it away. They bandaged up their bloody knees and called themselves clumsy. It often isn't until a major trauma occurs that we are forced to stop, look, and see the truth of the situation.

It was the onset of menopause that sent up cautionary flags for me, demanding that I slow down and pay attention to my body. Like many women, I ignored those first signals and maintained my intense schedule.

After crisscrossing the country for nine years conducting workshops, my body finally said "no more." I threw out my back, developed a case of shingles, was constantly nursing a cold or flu, and started to experience a crushing despair.

One day in the midst of a workshop, in some city I cannot even name, I experienced an intense power surge (*hot flash*, for the uninitiated). I commented to my all-female audience that perhaps these heat surges were nature's way of burning off the residue from our past and getting us prepared for the life ahead. (Could millions of women having hot flashes be causing global warming?) Maybe all the old self-limiting beliefs, behaviors and painful experiences of our lives were being turned to ash, becoming fertilizer for something new, something usable!

"After all, we each learn a great deal on our life journey. Through our experiences, we accrue wisdom and insight," I said, warming to the idea. "Surely there is a plan to transform and utilize these lessons to benefit both ourselves and our society. Dragging unhealed or unhealthy parts of ourselves into our future simply creates

The intuitive mind is a sacred gift and the rational mind is a faithful servant.

We have created a society that honors the servant and has forgotten the gift.

ALBERT EINSTEIN

a needless burden and promotes a sense of fatigue and dis-*ease* in one's body." At the time, I had no real appreciation for how spot-on this insight was!

This observation signaled the beginning of the end of my speaking career. But for "financial reasons" (read: fears) I paid no heed to the initial message and stayed too long. I soon reached the point where I really didn't want to talk to anybody—about anything. It all seemed so pointless. My moods were erratic, I had difficulty sleeping, I cried a lot and I felt a sense of loss and anxiety that I couldn't explain. My libido was non-existent and the only desire I had was to curl up in a ball and cocoon. I eventually came to appreciate that this major life transition required respect and attention, and I understood it was *so* much more than just a physical change.

You would think I might have learned my lesson! Years before, a similar thing had happened to me. My body had been sending me clues along the way that I had ignored. I pushed through many a symptom, thinking I was just lazy or tired or bored. Now I understand I was symptomatic because my life was off track and out of balance. I was working at a job I disliked. I was not setting clear or healthy boundaries in my marriage. I was struggling with how to hold together a blended family. I was stressed, had low self-esteem and carried a lot of internalized anger. I was living a lie, and my body was simply trying to get my attention so that I would make the changes necessary to put my life back on track.

My journey to understanding was delayed by my stubborn unwillingness to pay attention to these messages, which eventually culminated in major burnout (and a seven-year struggle with depression and chronic fatigue). Does any of this sound familiar to you?

Listening to Your Body

I learned the hard way that our bodies will manifest physically whatever is left unhealed emotionally. It was only by paying attention to the messages from within that I was able to make the changes necessary to reclaim my overall sense of health and well-being.

I discovered the body has a wisdom all its own and will tell us what it needs, what works, and what doesn't. While our heads can be thinking about the past or fantasizing about the future, our body is *always* in the present and will do whatever is necessary to ensure its survival. What may seem like a body gone out of control may in fact be a complex communication to your conscious mind. It's up to each of us to pay attention. By doing so, we are given an opportunity to make a new choice—the choice to stop, listen, heal, and redesign your life to one of your liking.

The body is a good place to start learning how to keep yourself company. Our physiology supports us in making the emotional and spiritual changes necessary to reconnect with our authentic center. Many of us haven't developed the habit of listening to our bodies. Like anything we want to excel at, this takes practice. Busyness can be a distraction, but ultimately your body will get your attention.

The body is a sacred garment. It is your first and last garment. It is what you enter life in, and what you depart with, and it should be treated with honor.
MARTHA GRAHAM

Sitting right where you are, close your eyes and take a few deep breaths. Pay attention to what your body is experiencing. *Fatigue? Headache? Body ache? Stiff knees? Heat? Stomach upset? Bloating? Calm? Sore back? Swollen glands? Tension? Relaxation?*

~ Jot down your experience.

~ Now, listen. What is your body trying to tell you? Write down the first thoughts that arise; do not edit or discard any information.

So many people spend their health gaining wealth, and then have to spend their wealth to regain their health.

A.J. REB MATERI

Examples:
You're not drinking enough water.
You're eating too much junk food.
You're doing a great job of taking time for yourself.
Girl, you're in menopause!
You're spending more than you're making.
You need to stretch more.
You need to devote more time to yourself.
You're hiding a secret.

_____

_____

_____

_____

_____

_____

~ First, acknowledge yourself for the ways in which you *do* take care of yourself.

~ Next, choose your most upsetting or troublesome symptom.

~ What is your body asking you to do differently, or more of? Close your eyes and listen.

~ List five ways it might benefit you to make the suggested changes.

~ Understanding the benefits, will you choose to implement this change into your life in the next 48 hours? If not, why not? *Who is making this decision?*

~ Solicit support from a friend to help you stay on track.

~ Write your commitment to yourself on index cards or sticky notes to constantly remind you to follow through on your promise. Breaking a promise to yourself starts a cycle of self-hate and, once more, your body will pay the price.

Check in with your body every day. Aging gracefully requires us to pay attention to the body's needs and make the adjustments that it asks for. When we listen and respond, we build health and vitality into this miraculous instrument that houses our precious life force. You'll also find it easier to establish and maintain meaningful relationships with others when you are centered and connected to yourself. Sounds like a good investment to me!

It pays to keep moving

For those who do not embrace a healthy, active lifestyle, the later years could be spent in an incapacitated state. In 2003, the *Journal of Gerontology*[14] published a study showing that the brains of physically fit people experienced less age-related shrinkage than those of less active people. Activity keeps your brain working, your body healthy and your bones strong.

After almost five years of minimal physical activity, low energy, depression, bloating and weight gain, I got off my duff and joined a gym. It was hard. For the first few weeks I just rolled around on the stability ball, complaining about my back. I eventually stopped whining, and I kept showing up. Now, I'm taking dance, Pilates and yoga classes. My energy levels have increased, and, because my core muscles have strengthened, my back and knee pain are long gone. I am stronger and more flexible, able to tote my grandkids and chase them around the park. Without dieting, I have dropped pounds of fat and gained muscle. The flotation device that mysteriously

Life is movement. The more life there is, the more flexibility there is. The more fluid you are, the more alive you are.
ARNAUD DESJARDINS

affixed itself around my middle in my fifties would no longer keep me afloat. I actually have a waistline again!

I actually feel more physically fit and energized than I did at 50. Putting aside my fears, I auditioned for—and got a dancing part in—a community theatre production. I am finishing up my first book (you're reading it!) and plan to facilitate workshops for women going through this wondrous but challenging next step. I am excited about life!

How about you?

What do you need to change, be, do or have in order to experience the life you want?

~ What is stopping you?

~ *Who* is stopping you?

_____

_____

_____

_____

_____

_____

_____

Remember, don't believe those voices, they are not on your side!

Uh-huh.

CHAPTER 7

Back to Your Roots

FOR MANY WOMEN, OUR initial confrontation with the physical evidence of aging comes on the day we spot that first wiry strand of gray hair. Initially we yank them out with a vengeance. After a while, many of us succumb to the endless routine of hair dye.

Once the process of coloring your hair begins, it takes on a life of its own. We try to coordinate our hair appointments with the events in our life. *Can I stretch it another week? There's that wedding coming up… when, in my busy schedule, can I find the time to have my hair dyed?* Our hair has its own budget, service person, brand… and it's a hassle! Eventually, some of us tire of that process and allow our silver lining to emerge.

Have you ever wondered why we don't keep our natural-born color till death do us part? Rest assured, it's not your partner's fault. It's genetics!

On average, a Caucasian woman begins to see gray hairs sprout around age 34, while an African American has 10 more years until she begins her vigil. By age 50, half of all women will be 50 percent gray.[15]

Most of us have about 100,000 hairs on our head, and each one of them started out full of a pigment called *melanin*. As hair develops in the follicle, melanin is deposited into the developing hair shaft by the pigment-producing cells of the skin, the *melanocytes*. The more melanin they produce, the darker the hair color.

As we age, melanocytes slow down their pigment production; eventually they stop altogether. Hair without melanin is actually transparent, but it takes on shading from the surrounding hair, which makes it seem gray. As more and more of these melanocytes stop working, the hair appears to get grayer and grayer, until finally it looks white.

It's interesting to note that melanocytes also produce the pigment in skin, and as they slow down with age, skin tone changes. It can look unnatural for a mature woman to wear the dark brown, deep red or honey blonde hair she had as a young woman. While the hair in and of itself looks lovely, it doesn't seem to go with her complexion or the character of her aging face. The wrong color hair with a woman's changing skin tone can make her look much older, exactly opposite of what she intends. Softer, lighter tones are usually the most flattering.

Are Hair Dyes Safe?

For some women, the safety of hair dye is a major consideration. For others it's not even on the radar screen. Because my body showed signs of distress whenever I colored my hair, I was motivated to find out more about hair dyes; what I learned through my research is downright scary.

The jury is still out regarding the safety of hair dye, weighing evidence that supports both sides of the argument. But here's something you should know: most hair dyes do *not* go through the same level of scrutiny as other cosmetic color additives.

According to the FDA, which does oversee the safety of most cosmetics sold in the United States and can prohibit the sale of those found to be harmful, they can't oversee and regulate the safety of most hair dyes. Why? The FDA can't regulate hair dye because it was originally made from coal tar.

What?!

Here's a little history: Back in the 1930s, coal tar, the primary ingredient in some hair dyes of the time, was causing an allergic reaction in some people. Concerned that the FDA could ban these hair dyes altogether, the industry successfully lobbied to exempt coal-tar hair dyes from the Food, Drug and Cosmetic Act of 1938, which gave the FDA the power to remove a product from the market if it was found to cause harm.[16]

So, if the FDA doesn't regulate hair dye, who's looking out for our safety? Until recently, the FDA relied on the cosmetics and fragrance industries to monitor themselves through an independent panel of industry experts. Who appoints them? The cosmetics industry! How stringent are these industry experts? Well, since 1976 this review board has found 694 ingredients safe and only 9 unsafe.[17] Hmmm.

In 1979, the hair-care industry adjusted the formula of most hair dyes to remove the primary cancer-causing agents. Many manufacturers of hair coloring products have removed some of the more toxic compounds that were shown to cause cancer in animals. That's the good news. The bad news is that they replaced them with ingredients that have a very similar chemical structure.

Is a Dye Job Worth Dying For?

Many scientific studies conducted since 1995 raise concerns about the ingredients in hair dyes.[18] Following is a brief overview of some of the more suspect ingredients of hair dye and some research into their safety. While it may seem a bit scientific, knowing what to look out for could save your life or the life of someone you love. As I get older, I find I can't read a lot of the product labels without a magnifying glass. If you have the same problem, don't let it stop you. March right up to the shelves with your magnifying glass in hand!

Coal tar, also known as P-phenylenediamine, is most often found in darker permanent hair dyes. Questions surrounding its safety have never been fully addressed. Another chemical ingredient, arylamine, has been linked to many conditions, from contact dermatitis, to eczema, to increased risk of bladder cancer.

Researchers at the University of Southern California, Keck School of Medicine found that individuals who used permanent hair dyes on a monthly basis for 15 years or more had *three times the risk* of bladder cancer of those who did not. One theory suggests that the hydrogen peroxide in the hair dye oxidizes certain molecules in the product and may set off pre-cancerous reactions in the body.[19]

The Cosmetic, Toiletry and Fragrance Association (CTFA) countered with a statement that questioned whether that data gathered in the USC study actually supported these conclusions.[20]

In April 2002, the USC Keck School of Medicine released data from another study that indicated women with the "NAT2 slow gene" tend to flush carcinogens out of their systems more slowly. This makes them more susceptible to bladder cancer. They looked at over 300 women with the NAT2 slow gene and found that those who used permanent hair dye had nearly tripled their risk of developing bladder cancer. (Increased risk was not seen in those who used temporary or semi-permanent dyes.)

Yale University researcher Tongzhang Zheng, ScD, also conducted a study that uncovered a correlation between hair dye and cancer. The results found that women who used dark hair dyes for more than 25 years, or used more than 200 applications of these products, doubled their risk of developing non-Hodgkin's lymphoma.[21]

The CTFA insists that the use of hair dyes does not elevate the health risk in women. They cite several well-designed epidemiologic studies conducted by the American Cancer Society and Harvard University, in which thousands of women were assessed and showed no elevated health risk related to using hair dyes.[22]

Dr. Zheng and colleagues note that there are two other large epidemiological studies that reached different conclusions. They take the position that all studies were limited by their methodologies, which may not have fully or accurately captured the level of exposure to hair dyes.[23]

So, whom do we believe? There seems to be a back and forth debate, and once again the consumer is left not knowing what to do!

If I only have one life to live, let me dye it as a blonde

For a while, blondes thought they were off the hook, since the toxins in question were only found in darker hair dyes. That illusion ended in September 2003, when the FDA's National Center for Toxicological Research reported the results of a new study. Using off-the-shelf hair-color products purchased in U.S. supermarkets and hair salons, they searched for a known carcinogen: 4-ABP. They found it in 8 of 11 hair dyes—shades of black, red and blonde.[24] Ironically, they didn't find it in brown shades.

What is really frightening about 4-ABP is that it is not an added ingredient. This cancer-causing toxin is a *by-product* of the dye-manufacturing process. Why is that relevant? Because you, the consumer, can't screen for this cancer-causing chemical—it's not an added ingredient, so it's not on the label.

The claims of the cosmetic industry that their products are safe remind me of the tobacco industry executives who testified over and over, in front of Congress and the American public, that cigarette smoking does not cause cancer.

Remember the researchers who found a higher risk of bladder cancer in women who used permanent hair dye? How did those chemicals end up in the bladder? According to the experts, it soaks into the body through the scalp. Our heads have numerous sweat glands, as well as the largest hair follicles and richest blood supply in the body. Hair dye is absorbed through the scalp, moved through the bloodstream, and eventually filtered to the bladder so the body can eliminate it. If you have the gene that slows down this process, the chemicals will take longer to clear your bladder, thereby increasing your risk of cancer.

To summarize…

- Very few studies have looked at the long-term (20+ years) safety of hair dyes, and few of those were double blind or controlled studies.
- The use of permanent hair coloring has been linked to non-Hodgkin's lymphoma, bladder cancer, leukemia and multiple myeloma.

- No studies have definitively linked breast cancer to hair dyes, although the link is suspected.

- Darker dyes carry a higher risk of causing cancer because of the increased number of chemicals, but blonde dyes also carry significant risk.

- While many dyes do not contain cancer-causing ingredients, the oxidizing process that occurs when the product is used may create cancer-causing chemicals.

It just seems logical to me that dyes with such questionable ingredients do not belong on our scalps, so close to our brains. If there is even a whiff of a chance to develop a life-threatening condition from coloring our hair, shouldn't we be looking for other options?

If our goal is truly to live long and healthy lives, it might be useful to question *why* we are willing to take these chemical risks.

We each have four choices: We can

1. Be genetically tested to see if we carry the NAT2 slow gene and make our decision to use hair dye accordingly
2. Take our chances and cross our fingers that we don't become ill from using hair dye
3. Use non-toxic hair coloring products
4. Opt to not color our hair at all

Yes, the cultural pressure to look young is powerful, but isn't your desire to live a long, healthy, authentic life even stronger?

"Natural" Options

Amazing Grays come in all colors—blonde, brunette, black, red, white and gray. I've noticed that dark-haired women tend to go silver, while those with lighter hair can develop a non-descript shade of gray. This makes sense if you remember that there is no such thing as *gray* hair. Hair devoid of melanin takes on the shading of the hairs around it. Darker hair colors reflect a silver tone, while the blonder shades reflect a yellow tone.

So, if having gray hair is not something you're ready to pursue (yet?), there are some healthful options to consider. Unfortunately, if you are currently using traditional chemical dyes, you cannot switch to natural coloring agents on the same dyed hair because of an adverse chemical reaction. You must grow your hair out and begin again with virgin hair, so to speak. (And you thought you could never be a virgin again!)

If you choose to color your hair with natural dye, be a wary shopper. Some of these self-professed "natural" hair dyes are really just toxic formulas packaged in a green box. There are some manufacturers that infuse their product with a few herbs and slap the word "natural" on the bottle, but these additives are often not enough to counter the toxicity of other ingredients.

Read the labels and watch for phenylenediamine, ammonia and resorcinol. These are not your friends.

Kim Erickson, author of *Drop-Dead Gorgeous*, wrote that virtually all mainstream cosmetic and personal care products contain hazardous chemical compounds; many contain more than one. In fact, of the roughly 5,500 substances approved for use in cosmetic and hygiene products, 884 were determined to be toxic by the National Institute of Occupational Safety and Health. That's 16 percent of their approved-substances list! Some are carcinogens. Some are neurotoxins. Some are hormone disruptors. Some cause organ damage.[25]

Do I have *some* of your attention?

Beyond the "approved" list, there is a long list of substances that are commonly used but not yet approved. As of June 2004, 89 percent (!) of the 10,500 ingredients used in face and body products have not been evaluated for safety by either the U.S. Food and Drug Administration or the cosmetics manufacturers.[26]

Ultimately, manufacturers are focused on the bottom line, and chemicals are often cheaper than natural ingredients. (But only if you ignore the long-term health cost.) While studies are often conducted to determine the short-term effects of a particular product, long-term studies are lacking. They simply don't impact the immediate profitability of the products.

For more information on the use of chemicals in personal care products and a list of products you might want to avoid, visit cosmeticsdatabase.com.

Natural hair colorings are mostly free of harmful synthetic chemicals. While these products are not effective at bleaching or lightning, they use color-rich plants to enhance hair color, bring out highlights, and tone down gray. Many women have had success coloring their hair or covering their gray by using chamomile (for blondes), sage, rosemary, walnut shells, tag alder bark, cloves and allspice rinses. These herbal remedies work progressively, adding a little more color every time you use them until you reach your desired shade. (Because of their progressive nature, they will obviously not lighten hair.) These herbal rinses are best used on un-dyed hair and are temporary to semi-permanent; they must be reapplied monthly to maintain the effect.

Henna is a plant that has been used for decades to color dark hair. Many natural ingredients can be added to enhance henna's color, including coffee, lemon juice, walnut shells, and rhubarb. Do not mix henna with chemical colorants or use it on hair that has already been chemically colored, as some unwanted colors and hair breakage may ensue. Henna has also been known to trigger asthma or other allergic reactions, so do a skin test first. After all, "natural" doesn't necessarily mean allergy free. Some people are allergic to strawberries, and how much more natural can you get?

Because of rising demand, new natural hair coloring products are now introduced regularly. Look for them at natural food stores or ask your hairstylist which plant-based hair dyes they are trained to use.

The Most Natural Option of All

My hairstylist tells me that many women over 50 have shared with her their desire to get off the never-ending cycle of coloring their hair and allow their natural silver lining to grow out. One reason many of them don't is that their husbands or partners don't want them to. This is a tough issue. If you decide to go naturally silver, your partner is forced to face the fact that he or she is getting older as well. Their internal picture of who they are is suddenly altered by their partner's silver hair. It reflects their own maturity back to them—a reality they might be reluctant to acknowledge. It's important to have an open discussion with your partner around your respective fears about getting older. Your acceptance of your maturing body (and hair) may help them to embrace their own. (And yours!) Unfortunately, there is a double standard in our society. Men are thought to look distinguished with silver hair, while women are thought to look old. Doesn't seem fair, does it? The only way to change these stereotypes is to challenge them.

For me, allowing my silver hair to emerge was the first step toward accepting my transition into a new chapter of my life. I was ready to let go of the ongoing effort to maintain the look of my youth—and ready to see what more life had to offer. I was looking forward to seeing who would emerge.

Like many women who struggle with this decision, I didn't have a clue *how* to go from colored hair back to natural again. I wasn't sure what was under all those chemicals, and I was a little frightened to find out! If that sounds familiar, this next chapter is for you.

CHAPTER 8

Becoming a Silver Sage

T HE TRANSITION FROM DYED hair to natural will be immeasurably easier if you do some internal work first. Take time to consciously embrace your decision to allow your hair to grow out—or at least embrace your willingness to *consider* going natural. Your inner voices of resistance will probably raise the roof, giving you all kinds of reasons why you should not proceed down this path.

What's going on inside your head?

∼ Write down what your inner voices are saying about allowing your silver lining to emerge. Give every last voice a chance to say its piece. (Then you get your peace.)

Examples:

I'll look like my grandma!
Gray hair is one step away from the grave.
I'll be ugly.
I'll lose my sex appeal.
I'll be invisible.

I won't be seen as powerful, capable or intelligent.
It means the end of my youth as I know it.
It means... I'm old!

Come on… these are all lies! None of us has a sexpiration date.

Are you willing to acknowledge that these are, once again, the fears of your conditioning, and simply "uh-huh" them and move on? Continuing to listen to them will just keep you stuck and unable to take action. These are the very same voices that have tormented you for years. Do *not* believe them; they are not on your side.

As I allowed my silver hair to emerge, I was haunted by these same messages. Having completed the process, I can testify that only one of these fears has proven to be true. When in the company of much younger people, I notice that they sometimes look right through me, as if I'm invisible. At first it was disconcerting, and I wondered if I had some embarrassing traces of lunch on my chin. After giving my mouth a discrete swipe and witnessing no change in their behavior, it hit me. They were simply reacting according to their conditioned beliefs about ladies with gray hair. Was I going to allow *their* conditioning to destroy *my* peace of mind? No way! What they think or don't think about me has nothing to do with my worth as a woman, and I give them no power in my life. I get to choose my own experience, and I choose self-acceptance.

Now, when I encounter a young person who is unable to really see me, I simply smile and walk away. If I'm being

If death meant just leaving the stage long enough to change costume and come back as a new character... Would you slow down? Or speed up?
CHUCK PALAHNIUK

ignored in a retail environment, I walk right up, make eye contact with the salesperson, and ask for what I want. A smile seems to be a universal connector.

There are always bumps in the road when we make a change. I found when I was centered and didn't give a flip about what other people thought about me, I felt *seen*—by me! And that's what matters most. I love my silver hair, and I look nothing like my grandma!

Bye-Bye Toxic Dye

Many women wonder *how* to go from colored hair to natural without going through a half-and-half stage. Sometimes there is no way around it. When faced with this dilemma, I explored various options and found four effective solutions.

Option #1: Wear a wig until you have enough new growth to cut off the dyed hair

I visited several wig shops and mall kiosks. For a small fee at most mall kiosks, you can sample several wigs to try out different styles and colors. The "silver" wigs I tried on looked ghastly on me, so I decided to stick with my own brown tones. I found several attractive wigs made with synthetic hair that cost between $80 and $150.

After much deliberation, I finally decided against a wig. I'm sensitive to pressure on my head, and being in the midst of menopause, it was just too hot for me… but it may be perfect for you!

We usually don't notice great-looking wigs on women because they look so natural; but the poorly chosen versions seem to scream *help! Mistake!* My advice is to take a friend with you who is not afraid to tell you the truth about what looks natural on you.

Option #2: Add lowlights to your hair as the silver grows in

This technique is also called "reverse highlights." When highlighting hair, the hairstylist teases out strands of hair throughout your head using a cap or sheets of foil; these strands are then lightened to give hair the sun-kissed look of youth. Highlighting silver hair tends to wash it out and make it look yellowed, so lowlights are preferred. Lowlights are done in the same manner as highlights, but darker colors are applied to the pulled strands. Because "gray" hair is really transparent and takes on the color of the surrounding hair, lowlights create a darkening effect. You can lowlight less and less hair with time, and gradually allow more and more of the silver to grow in, until you cut yourself free from the foil and join the ranks of the silver sages.

Option #3: Shave your head and let your hair grow out

It could happen. I read about a popular television star who shaved her head on her 50th birthday and allowed her silver hair to become her crowning glory. Because shaving gives you a smooth head, it might make it easier to wear a wig. If you choose to shave your head, I recommend you have a professional hairdresser or a friend help you. It makes quite a statement.

Option #4: Wait out the new growth and cut your hair short

Allow your natural hair to grow out an inch or two and then have it cut and styled into a short, attractive hairdo. Most people's hair grows at the rate of about ¼ to ½ inch per month. While you wait out the new growth, you can cover the most obvious showings along your part line and temples with a temporary coloring. Hair mascara is available at beauty supply stores in various shades that blend in with your hair color. It is inexpensive and can be used on the most visible roots, your part line and temples. It washes out (leaving a bit of residue) and must be reapplied daily, but it really covers the gray. There is a new hair color available, made just for roots, which also washes out. It costs a little more, but you simply dab it onto the roots and let it dry.

Which to choose?

I chose option #4. I estimated it would take four to six months before I had enough new growth to support an attractive haircut. Having enjoyed longer hair for years, I was a little unsure about cutting it *that* short. Going short and silver meant leaping into seniordom in one fell swoop, or so the inner voices of doom told me. I heard all about how I'd be marginalized, invisible and even unattractive, but I realized I had a choice to buy into this myth or not. I worked on it while my hair grew out, before I made the cut.

I used hair mascara for the first few months to hide the most obvious snowy showings. The last two months were another matter. As my hair grew out, applying hair mascara to long roots became more difficult, with hair getting tangled up in the brush and breaking off. It also took a *lot* more product to cover a *lot* more gray hair. And a stiff wind could undo in a moment all that I had done to disguise my roots. This is the point where you might want to get creative with hats and scarves.

Experiment, be bold. You're a boomer! Take a chance on yourself. Join the ranks of silver sages and let's make a statement. It's a risk worth taking. Remember, this process is reversible. If you grow your hair out to its natural silver luster and you really don't like it, you can always modify your look using one of the less toxic options. At least you will be free to choose the look and product you *want*, instead of the one mandated by your fears.

It's Not Easy Being Seen

In the midst of allowing my silver lining to emerge, I finally got tired of hiding the process. I challenged myself to step out and bare my considerable roots to the light of day. While some women are appalled at the idea of showing their "skunk line," I wanted to explore the feelings and issues that arose as I took my process public. By paying attention to the gremlins inside my head, the voices that constantly reaffirm my inadequacy, I hoped to expose my insecurities and reclaim my power. I certainly got my wish.

My husband and I went out to dinner on a Friday evening. We had to wait for our table, and the waiting area was bustling with people. I had about an inch and a half of silver growth atop my dyed brown bob, and I suddenly felt very self-conscious. I just knew everyone was looking at my silver roots and passing judgment on me. I saw many women do a double take, and I imagined them saying things like, "Doesn't she know her roots are showing? Doesn't she care enough about herself to go to her hairdresser? Look at all the snow on the roof! Who does she think she's fooling? What's that handsome man doing with such an unattractive older woman? Doesn't she look in the mirror? Poor thing." Of course, no one actually said a thing to me.

I sat in the darkest corner and actually felt ashamed! I felt like an outcast, like I was doing something wrong. I was taken aback by my intense reaction. I felt naked. Once again I felt the cultural pressure to be in style, look good, and above all, look young. Going against the social

Masquerading as a normal person day after day is exhausting.
ANONYMOUS

Your outer world is at every moment mirroring back to you your deepest feelings about yourself. If you don't like what you see "out there," the only place you can change it is within you.
DEBBIE FORD

norm can threaten those who are invested in maintaining the status quo, and they can get nasty when the rules are broken. After all, a society only holds together if everyone follows the rules.

It's easy to forget that most of what we think other people are saying or thinking is really just a projection of what we think about ourselves. All the fears I harbored about growing old, looking old, and being old I had projected onto others, believing they were thinking these thoughts about me.

What do you believe other people will say about you if you allow your hair to go gray?

∼ Make a list.

_____

_____

_____

By holding our fears up to the light of day we can render the voices of self-deprecation helpless.

Even though this was a conscious experiment on my part, the rush of self-deprecating emotions and thoughts absolutely shocked me. As I sat in that restaurant, a lifetime of programming about how one *should* look and behave descended like a fog. I finally looked at my husband and whispered, "*Help!*" By talking through my feelings and thoughts, I was able to release the negativity and see the programming and cultural standards for what they are—not true and not me.

The truth of that situation was simple. I was: 1) a woman who had decided not to color her hair any longer, 2) in the middle of the growing-out process, and 3) someone who had made a decision to not stay home and hide out until it was over.

That's *it.*

Father Time is not always a hard parent, and, though he tarries for none of his children, often lays his hand lightly upon those who have used him well; making them old men and women inexorably enough, but leaving their hearts and spirits young and in full vigor. With such people the grey head is but the impression of the old fellow's hand in giving them his blessing, and every wrinkle but a notch in the quiet calendar of a well-spent life.

CHARLES DICKENS

We are given countless opportunities to examine our beliefs about aging and decide whether or not they serve us in being our authentic self. Allowing other people's real or imagined opinions to matter so much makes us victims. To reclaim our power, we each have to take responsibility for the beliefs we hold—and accept or change them.

Since going silver, I've noticed there is a special camaraderie between women who proudly sport a head full of silver hair. When we meet, we often exchange smiles and nod, as if we've discovered some little secret that others are missing out on. I think we may be on to something!

Making the Final Cut

After five months of wrestling with hair mascara and my fears about getting older, I made an appointment to have my hair trimmed. On the day of the appointment, my hairstylist commented that there was actually enough new growth to create a short but attractive style. I could become the silver fox I was aiming to be—right then and there!

Time stopped. My eyes widened as I realized what that meant. I began mumbling all the reasons why I was not quite ready. I offered excuses about why we should wait (though, to this day I can't remember what they were). She pulled up my roots and showed me how much silver growth I really had. I waffled back and forth. My life flashed before my eyes. (Well, not really, but it lends an air of drama.) Finally, I took a deep breath and said, "Go ahead." She quickly grabbed a handful of hair and made a deep cut before I could change my mind.

There was no going back… this was it.

I'd never seen her cut hair so quickly. She was clearly aware of the potential for trauma and proceeded as if she

A smile is the lighting system of the face, the cooling system of the head, and the heating system of the heart.

UNKNOWN

My own growing out process

1: A salon visit covers the gray but leaves those golden highlights I was so attached to.

2: After 3 months, my roots are waaaay past the point where I always had them re-dyed.

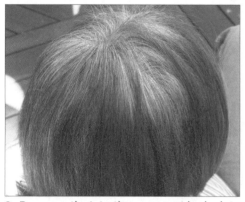

3: Four months into the process, I had a lot of snow on the roof!

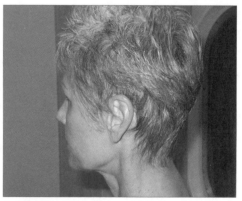

4: The Final Cut. I was still in shock!

were on a mission. I thank her for that. It was like pulling off a bandage: the quicker, the better.

The experience was surprisingly liberating. As each handful of artificially colored hair piled up on the floor around me, I felt freed from a part of me that I no longer identified with. I felt as though I was becoming lighter, which in a metaphorical sense was exactly what was happening. The weight of trying to be who I thought I *should* be was slowly lifted from my shoulders, and the authentic me started to emerge. Outgrown standards of beauty dropped to the floor, and I stood on the threshold of a new phase of life.

That day I saw the face of an elder emerge, with eyes shining (perhaps it was tears?) and *very* short silver hair tipped with wisps of brown. I kind of liked how she looked.

My inner voices, however, wouldn't allow *that* to go on for long. I suddenly panicked and the voices inside me screamed, "What have you done? This is horrible! You look *old*!" I thanked Pam and rushed out of the salon, hurrying home to hide.

Once home, I ran into the bathroom and locked the door. Thankfully, my husband was outside cutting the grass, so I had some time to myself to process this huge change. I stared at the stranger in the mirror. She looked so different than the image I was used to seeing; it was truly like looking at someone else. I could see the distress on her face. I had to talk her down.

I looked deeply into her eyes and slowly, gradually, through the tears I found the person I was looking for. I coaxed her out and breathed her back to center. Once there, we admired the cut. Short, but rather sassy. The silver color was actually quite lovely. It suited her. I smiled and reassured her that everything was all right. She smiled back.

Finally, I was able to claim her as me.

Suddenly there was a knock at the door. "Why is the door locked?" my husband asked. I took another deep breath and asked him if he was ready to meet his new wife, the silver fox. I slowly opened the door and (bless that man) he *loved* it! He thought I had never looked so beautiful, and he gave me a hug that allowed me to let go. I felt free, authentic, beautiful and very, very loved.

The whole process of going silver threw me back onto myself and encouraged me to come to grips with the baggage I'd been carrying around about getting (and looking) older. It's a decision I have never regretted as it was the first step toward reclaiming my authenticity. I now know that my joy and happiness are not dependent on the reactions, feelings or opinions of those around me. I am accountable for my own experience. My state of being comes from inside of me.

If you decide to make the switch, I invite you to track your experience of allowing your silver lining to grow out.

~ Have someone take a "before" picture of you.

~ Write a short paragraph about why you have decided to allow your silver lining to come forth.

~ Be mindful of what the inner voices are telling you, remembering they are not your friends. Uh-huh.

~ Talk over your decision with your partner or a friend, ask for their support and allow them to express their concerns. If they can't support you, find someone who can.

~ Keep a journal of your experience and take photos along the way. If you wish, send your digital "after" picture and a 300-word story about your experience to the gallery of silver sages at *www.maggiecrane.com.*

I look forward to meeting you there!

Gallery of Silver Sages

Many women love to hear about others women's experiences. In these shared exchanges we find inspiration, courage, ideas and a sense of connection.

The following pages present a sampling of stories from women who have had enough of dyeing their hair and have taken the leap into authenticity.

CATHLEEN FRANK
(b. 1957)

IT JUST OCCURRED TO me the other day that out of all my friends, I am the only one who does *not* color her hair any longer!

As a Pilates instructor, I have always tried to model good health and wellness. When my gray started to come in, I was encouraged by those close to me to "take care of it." And so I did, for nine years.

Truth is, I hated coloring my hair! Not only were all those trips to the salon costly, I could never count on leaving with the color I came in with. The stains on my neck, ears, and temples were often embarrassing. It honestly never occurred to me that "going gray" was an option until just two years ago—when I saw Joanne.

Joanne had been a student of mine whom I hadn't seen in years. She had been a slightly overweight, jolly woman with thick, waist-length hair flecked with gray. One day, I spotted her husband, only recognizing Joanne because she was standing beside him. She was stunning! Her short, silver hair was fashionably spiked; she had dropped 40 pounds and looked long, lean and elegant. She now exuded sereneness, a quiet dignity, and an inner knowingness. Then, she shared with me that she was a breast cancer survivor. I was humbled and deeply touched. I had a hero.

I never went back to my hairdresser. I was ready to experience the *privilege* of growing older. Going gray was simply the first step.

My gray came in beautifully and I love it! I still get compliments from women who seem amazed that gray hair can be so attractive. When I was coloring my hair, I felt flawed and inauthentic. Once I went gray, that facade melted away and "the real me" was revealed. I cut my hair VERY short like my hero, Joanne, and immediately felt sassy and confident. I began wearing less makeup, and I didn't feel compelled to explain myself—to anyone, about anything. The filter that had previously protected "me" from "others" dissolved and my heart opened up. I became a better listener and friend. I was passionate about my career once again. I felt strong. I broke free from the competitive "youth oriented" nature of my career and began to specialize in programs for women of a "certain age."

Fitness is real. You either do it or you don't, and the results are obvious. So few things are real. My daughter is 15. She knows that my silver hair and the lines on my face are evidence of a life that has seen some challenges, some blood, some gore, some great stories, and some effort! What is "real" isn't always pretty and it's never easy. My job as her mother is to be an example of what is real by how I live, what I believe and how I love. Nothing else really matters.

Cathleen, a Pilates Master Trainer, has been an athletic trainer for 20 years. Her specialty is designing fitness "lifestyles" for men and women over 40, incorporating her "no nonsense" approach to fitness, attention to biomechanics and motivational coaching techniques.

Eileen Bennett
(b. 1951)

My hair was controlling my life—and hairdressers were controlling my hair. Every three weeks I spent several hours at the salon, trying to look "natural." To maintain the look, I tried to avoid the sun, the beach and swimming. I washed my hair as little as possible and often wore a hat to protect the color.

My hair always looked great the first week after it was colored. Beyond that, it would start fading and my silver roots would start showing—what a joke! There had to be a better way. Periodically, I would get one of those new shades mixed in "to jazz up my face," like that burgundy tint added to brown or a nice red touch. Ugh! They were so unnatural and added a harshness that made me look more comical that youthful. Who was I trying to kid?

I was turning 50 and felt good—except for all the hassles with my hair.

While on vacation, I noticed two strikingly attractive women with silver hair. They exemplified refinement, vitality, good health and confidence. The color of their hair in no way diminished the youthfulness of their healthy appearance. I was impressed, and so was my husband. This was the look I wanted.

With these women in mind, I decided to go silver. It took several tries before I found a color specialist who would see me through the transition. My regular stylist was not supportive, saying that gray was usually not attractive and that most women were not happy with their natural color. How wrong she was.

First, my new colorist removed as much of the artificial color as she could from my brown hair. Then she added back a lighter shade. For the first time in my life, I was a blonde! I stayed blonde for the next year, gradually going from a full head of color to just streaking it as the silver grew in. Because I wear my hair long, it took about 18 months to complete the process.

I love my hair! My natural color is not only becoming, it is healthier and shiner that my overly conditioned colored hair ever was. Experts told me that my hair would be coarse and dull when it grew in. Not so! My silver hair is like silk, and I've been able to toss out my expensive hair products.

There seems to be a "club" of women who have allowed their silver to emerge. Our club does not reflect the stereotypical gray-haired grandmother. When we make eye contact, we recognize a kindred spirit; someone who had confidently accepted her maturity and embraces being a proud, vital, attractive, *active* women. Being young is a state of mind, not a look. I am as young as I feel, and, as ironic as it sounds, silver hair has made me feel younger than I did when I spent so much time trying to cover it up.

Eileen has a degree in chemistry and worked as a research chemist and a regulatory analyst. She is married and has two children. She loves to travel and considers life an adventure.

Lynn Colwell
(b. 1945)

I NOW HAVE WHITE HAIR. Half a dozen years ago, I was a blonde. Before that, a brunette. When, at age 57, I finally decided to embrace my natural color, it was an act of both practicality and courage.

On the practical side, my hair grows faster than bamboo. I'd spend an entire afternoon and a lot of money getting it colored and by the weekend, white tendrils were springing up around my face like wildflowers after the rain. Every couple of weeks I'd have to do "touch-ups," which were messy, smelly and difficult.

On the courage side, what red-blooded baby boomer wants to look old? That's what everyone assumes if you have white hair. You might as well go around wearing a Medicare t-shirt!

One day, after a bottle of hair dye slipped from my hand and sprayed the entire bathroom with shards of broken glass and globs of Medium Golden Blonde, I had an awakening.

First, I sat down in the middle of the mess and cried. While making a feeble attempt to clean up, I started thinking about why I was coloring my hair. Who was I doing it for? What was I gaining from the process and what would I lose if I stopped?

These were daunting questions I'd never considered before. I'd been dyeing my hair since my 20s. I wondered what it might be like to show who I am at this moment to the world. Would I be treated differently? How would I feel about myself if I moved against the tide? Would my hair be the beautiful white my mother-in-law called her crowning glory? Or the gray of a worn-out building? And would it matter?

I noodled on these questions until the day I was accepted into graduate school, pursuing my goal of a master's degree in counseling. I knew that the program would involve much self-exploration, and I surmised that if I expected my future clients to be completely real with me, I would have to "get real" with myself.

Letting my hair go natural became the external symbol of that monumental decision. I was pledging to be honest, to be fully myself and to deal with the consequences from the core of my being.

I find that in some venues I am invisible and in others, unique. Instead of getting upset when a salesperson ignores me (which they do all the time), I simply walk up and ask for what I want. The quick looks or lack of them, the assumptions made in a second's glance, have fueled my natural inclination to disprove stereotypes.

White hair has allowed me to experience life in a different, new, challenging, even fun way. It has forced me to acknowledge not who I wish I was, but who I am. I love it when a young person says that knowing me has helped erase some of their fear of aging. If you worry about what people will think about you if you break from the norm, consider what you may discover about yourself as you make the choice to go silver. You may be surprised!

(Edited and reprinted with permission from the author.)

Lynn Colwell has had a varied career, from childbirth educator to corporate communications. She now serves as a life coach. She has been married to the same man for 39 years.

Charlotte O'Brien
(b. 1950)

FOLLOWING IN MY MOTHER's footsteps, I began going gray in my late thirties. My silver streak continued to widen, and when I was 40, a hairdresser stopped me on the street and exclaimed, "Your hair color is beautiful—I hope you never dye it!" Her kind remark validated my sense that the silver color suited me.

Then my mother died. Suddenly, the silver streak seemed to be an unwanted reminder that I would be following in her footsteps again soon enough. So, before I gave the eulogy at her funeral, and in an effort to look young, I colored my hair and erased all traces of silver.

To maintain my dark hair, it was necessary to color it every three weeks! What a bother. It was obvious to anyone who looked that I was going gray—fast. Finally, I just had enough. What was the point, and who was I trying to fool? At age 52, I decided to allow my silver to grow back in.

To accelerate the process, I had my long hair cut short. My silver hair is a different texture than my dark hair was, and it is better suited to a short style—so I've kept it that way. My husband also prefers it short—he thinks my neck and shoulders are sexy. Can't argue with that.

My women friends love my hair. They think I'm really brave. I don't think of myself as brave. I just don't want to ever be a slave to what someone else thinks I should look like. I get a lot of inquisitive—as well as admiring—looks from women, especially at the salon. I think a lot of them would like to stop coloring their hair, but either don't feel ready or are unsure of what color they'll end up with. Men still look. Boys too. Sometimes I think they think they see a blonde, and then, oops, no—it's someone my mom's age! Oh no!

For a while, I was concerned that having silver hair might limit my options. I didn't want to stay in my current job for another 15 years just because I was *afraid* I could never get another! No way. So rather than get stuck there out of fear—I quit. If I do go back to work for someone else, I know that I won't be coloring my hair again. If I don't get hired, I'll just hire myself!

Charlotte has an MA in Fine Arts and spent one term as president of her local Soroptimist Club. She also served as manager for the California Strawberry Festival for five years. She and her husband of 25 years have one daughter.

∞

To read more about the women who are shucking off the trappings of hair dye and reclaiming their authenticity, visit *www.maggiecrane.com*. If and when you are ready to join us, please consider submitting your short story and photo as well.

PHOTO BY ROBIN REID

Me on my 60th birthday

CHAPTER 9

Riding the Cycle

S IF GOING GRAY weren't enough to challenge our mettle, once again we women are faced with raging hormones. It's like being an adolescent all over again! (With privileges, of course.)

I learned that throughout our lives, our hormones fire in different combinations, at different intensities, and for differing amounts of time, creating a wide range of effects on our brains, bodies and emotions, and facilitating our progression through the various chapters of our lives. Nature is not random, and everything that goes on in our bodies is purposeful.

Right around puberty, girls often go from tomboys to tomcats. This is not bad, and again, not random—it's hormones! They biologically prepare us to attract a mate, bear children and nurture our families. In a sense, we are hormonally scripted to fulfill our roles.

During our fertile years, the body continues to produce hormones that create feel-good sensations of calm, warmth and satisfaction.[27] Nature probably designed it to feel this good so that women would be encouraged to continue being caretakers, thus assuring the nurturance of their families.

Then, typically in our early forties, things begin to shift. Suddenly we feel a range of emotions that we didn't feel before—or didn't allow ourselves to feel. *Peri*menopause enters our lives and turns the basket upside down, dumping our sanity and peace of mind onto the floor. For many, it's like exaggerated PMS. We feel like moody adolescents again, but now we also have night sweats, low libido, and sometimes, even depression to deal with! Some of us are still raising children; many are busy with careers; and most of us have more on our plates than we can healthfully manage.

Somewhere in our late forties or early fifties, the sporadic and occasional shift in hormones that marks perimenopause finally gives way to a steady diet of symptoms that can no longer be ignored or easily dealt with. *Symptoms of low estrogen include:*

Hot flashes	Mental fuzziness
Night sweats	Headaches
Low libido	Vaginal dryness
Fatigue	Incontinence
Mood swings	Infections of the bladder

Sound familiar? If so, you are most likely in menopause. If you're anything like me, you might find yourself frantically trying to press the "pause" button on life as you sweat your way through busy days and sleepless nights. A strange feeling of anxiety starts to creep in, and you find yourself wondering what the heck is going on! More than you know.

When it finally dawned on me that menopause was fast approaching, I read everything about it I could get my (sweaty) hands on.

While I have always trusted my intuitive sense of the purposeful seasons of a woman's life, Dr. Christiane Northrup's book *The Wisdom of Menopause* reinforced my own understandings. As a medical doctor, she put research and professional expertise behind things that I had always sensed but not been credentialed to prove. In her book, she writes:

> *Research into the physiological changes taking place in the perimenopausal woman is revealing that, in addition to the hormonal shift that means the end to childbearing, our bodies—and specifically, our nervous systems—are being, quite literally, rewired. It's as simple as this: Our brains are changing. A woman's thoughts, her ability to focus, and the amount of fuel going to the intuitive centers in the temporal lobes of her brain all are plugged into, and affected by, the circuits being rewired.*[28]

So I wasn't going crazy!

From Transition to Transformation

Through my research (and experience!), I learned that hormone fluctuations strongly affect the way one sees and experiences the world, and they are the driving force behind the changes taking place in a midlife woman's brain. One cycle of life is giving way to another. The hormonal veil that kept us invested in the responsibilities of hearth and home is gradually lifted. We are compelled to look deep within to ready ourselves for what is coming by releasing the unhealed bits and beliefs that no longer support us in moving forward.

There is also a desire to find purposeful work and meaning in one's own life that is not predicated on the immediate care of others. We become less tolerant, feel less nurturing, express strong emotions more readily, feel a little irritated and want more time alone. If we continue to ignore or resist the messages, our bodies will often manifest our discontent through physical illness or mental distress.

The causal relationship between our emotional states and physical illness is well documented. People who die from a sudden heart attack often lived lives in which they were unable to express anger or hostility; they suffered from a hardened heart, if you will. Several medical studies link breast cancer to a woman's feeling of powerlessness in key relationships or being unable to fully express herself emotionally.[29]

It has become evident that our female hormones are not solely for reproduction. After all, if that were the case, they would disappear once that childbearing phase of life was over. I'll let Dr. Northrup explain:

> It would seem that your body, in its wisdom, has ulterior motives for continuing to produce the so-called reproductive hormones, when reproduction no longer is the point.... Estrogen and progesterone molecules bind themselves to areas such as the amygdala and hippocampus, which are important for memory, hunger, sexual desire, and anger. Changing levels of these and other hormones may well help to bring up old memories, accompanied by strong emotions, especially anger. This is not to say that anger is caused by hormonal change. Rather, it means that the hormonal change simply facilitates remembering and clearing up unfinished business.[30]

In the end, our reproductive hormones are not only there to help us give birth to our babies, but to help us give birth to *ourselves*!

Could the hormonal "curse" (as so many of us called it) really be a blessing in disguise? Each month, as the hormones rage and the blood flushes from our bodies, difficult emotions often arise. We can feel angry, irritable, weepy or tired. Rather than just accept *"this is how I feel at that time of the month,"* perhaps we might ask if our hormones are conspiring to provoke us into looking at things we have tucked away in our unconscious. We are prodded to revisit these issues and heal them, once and for all.

To the extent that you ignore your opportunities to clean house, these issues will accumulate over the years. Eventually, these unhealed issues arise with more fire and force than before. As women move closer to menopause, they are often bothered by past traumas that they haven't thought of in years, and become increasingly disturbed by the injustices they see in the world.

So no, you're not going crazy either!

After a while, it takes more effort to resist these issues than to let them go, and most of us come to terms with the understanding that the only way out—is through.

The first step to wisdom is silence; the second is listening.
UNKNOWN

Take a moment to observe your feelings.

~ The next time you experience a hot flash, anxiety or generalized PMS, sit still and become an observer. Give yourself time and permission to process the feelings that are simmering below the surface. Ride the wave of heat or emotion without becoming it, and look to see what issues are coming up for you.

Examples: *Career, empty nest, difficulty in your relationship(s), fear of growing older, injustice, too many demands on your time, expectations from others, etc.*

~ Choose the issue that bubbles to the surface first—yes, *that* one!

~ Do whatever you feel drawn to do: observe, cry, wail, journal, paint, move, renegotiate a relationship, set healthier boundaries, make a plan to spend time alone.

~ Embrace the difficulty and look for the gift or message in it. Can you see it as an opportunity for a deeper awareness?

~ Picture a dear friend coming to you for advice on that issue. What would your compassionate self tell her?

~ Can you heed your own advice?

~ Hold the challenge in your heart and imagine your body heat turning it into ashes, transforming its energy to help you embrace a new understanding.

~ What happened to your anxiety or hot flash as you allowed the issues to surface?

Trust yourself—you are adequate to your experience!

Taking the time to journal these and related questions may provide you with the insight necessary to heal lingering issues, allowing you to tap into the deep well of energy available as you transition and turn your golden years to silver.

Women who don't take the time to honor their mini wake-up calls along the way typically have more pronounced PMS symptoms and experience greater difficulty throughout menopause. The more unhealed issues one has, the tougher these transitions can be, simply because there is more to be uncovered, expressed and resolved.

As we become more aware and move toward the things that bring us joy, we actually create new neural pathways in the brain. Right-brain function, which is responsible for connection, creativity, emotion and imagination, actually continues to grow as women age. Our intuitive abilities are honed and our proficiency at grasping the big picture and seeing the whole is enhanced.[31]

Once again, to aid the process of moving on, we must let go of what was in order to be open to what is. Joan Borysenko writes in *A Woman's Book of Life*:

> *While each stage builds upon previous biology and experience, evolving from one stage to the next sometimes requires a dying to what we have been in order to complete our metamorphosis…. Older women are supposed to fade graciously—or gloomily—into the woodwork. Yet, as studies demonstrate, the truth is that women continue to develop their strengths and actually bloom, rather than fade, with the advent of midlife.*[32]

We can bury our heads in the sand and pretend it's not happening, even numb ourselves with medication… or, we can consciously embrace the opportunity to handle whatever arises. Each stage of life prepares us for the next. The more consciousness you bring to the process, the easier it is to ride the cycle. While it looks different for each of us, this hormonal adventure is simply another loop in the feminine life cycle.

If this is where you find yourself—congratulations! The next stage of your life has begun, and there's so much more to it than just raging hormones. But we'll start there.

And So It Begins

Perimenopause, a period of hormone fluctuation that is actually the precursor to menopause, begins, on average, sometime in our early- to mid-forties. A lot is going on here: Not only are our bodies changing, but our brains are being rewired too. Many women (including me) start to experience temporary but crazy-making symptoms such as sleeplessness, anxiety, night sweats and heart palpitations. Our hormone levels begin to vacillate, gradually becoming more erratic as the years go by. Typically, a drop in progesterone precipitates these initial symptoms. I remember waking in the middle of the night with my heart pounding and becoming frightened. I thought I must be having a heart attack or coming down with a major illness. My doctor assured me this physical chaos was all perfectly normal at this stage of life, and I was able to put aside my worry.

Throughout our adult lives, there is a dynamic balance between progesterone and estrogen. Estrogen is important for almost everything that makes you a woman. Progesterone plays a critical role in preparing the uterus to support a pregnancy. When the brain gets the signal that no embryo is present, progesterone levels drop and the uterine lining is sloughed off as a monthly period.

Progesterone also affects brain function, acting as a calming sedative and allowing us to sleep more deeply. It's no surprise that falling levels of this important hormone can produce sleepless nights and unexplainable bouts of anxiety. Because progesterone levels drop more rapidly than estrogen at this time in life, the delicate balance is upset, leaving women with excess estrogen. Often, a natural progesterone supplement will restore the hormonal balance and symptoms disappear. There are also some simple lifestyle changes and natural remedies that can help smooth out these physical speed bumps: a change in diet, herbal infusions, increased exercise, and a little more time for ourselves. If you're in the throes of perimenopause, you might consider having your hormone levels assessed. Talk with your doctor to discuss your options and explore natural alternatives to synthetic hormones. Over-the-counter preparations of progesterone are available, but oftentimes the doses are questionable. Partnering with a healthcare practitioner well versed in bio-identical options will help you determine the best approach for you.

The Real Deal: Menopause

It's difficult to say *exactly* when menopause begins and ends, as it typically occurs over a 10-15+ year continuum (including the initial perimenopausal years). It creeps up slowly and envelops you in its warm embrace before you know what's happening. The official beginning of full-blown menopause is marked by twelve consecutive months without a menstrual period. (Typically, a complete hysterectomy will throw you into menopause as well.)

Once you experience plunging hormone levels, then the fun really begins (she said facetiously)! Suzanne Somers describes this experience to a tee in her book, *The Sexy Years*:

> …the Seven Dwarfs of Menopause arrived at my door without warning: Itchy, Bitchy, Sweaty, Sleepy, Bloated, Forgetful and All-Dried-Up. One by one they crept into my own private cottage in the woods and started to take over my life. The first to arrive was Itchy. I developed this itch on my calf that was so irritating, I wanted to scratch the skin right off my

body. Then Bitchy came to my door. No longer was my PMS contained to one or two days a month—it felt like constant PMS. Then I would swing from Bitchy to weepy—for God's sake, what was wrong with me?

Ding-dong... It's the middle of the night, and Sweaty has crawled into bed with me. Oh, yes, Sweaty brought embarrassing hot flashes and introduced me to night sweats, where it seemed as if a faucet had been attached between my breasts. Of course, Sweaty brought about Sleepy because I was tired all the time. I would wake up so many times in the night and not be able to get back to sleep. Bloated crept in slowly. My once-svelte figure got thick through the middle section, even though I was following my weight-loss program that had worked so well for so many years! I can't remember when Forgetful arrived, but one day my brain stopped working. I considered myself a pretty focused woman until Forgetful came and I could not keep a coherent thought in my brain.... Am I getting Alzheimer's? I wondered. Last, All-Dried-Up slowly encroached upon my happy marriage. This was probably the most unpleasant of the dwarf family. Sex was no longer on the top of my list... or on my list at all. My husband would give me that knowing look, and I would think, "Frankly, I'd rather have a smoothie."[33]

Can you relate? My "Itchy" felt more like ants crawling up my legs, but close enough.

They don't call it meno*pause* for nothing.

Give yourself permission to revise and revamp your life to make way for the coming changes. After ignoring my body's signals for years—and enduring the unpleasant results—I slowly began to acknowledge the wisdom in them. I finally honored my body's call for help and made a conscious decision to press the "pause" button on my life. It was one of the most grounded, self-respecting decisions I could have made.

I stopped traveling and changed my work schedule, and I made fewer commitments. I wasn't checking out; I was slowing down. I was simplifying my life in order to create a space for something new. Most importantly, I began to quiet my mind and listen. After all, you cannot fill a pail with fresh water when the bottom is full of mud.

Menopause is a time to burn off old ways of doing and being, uproot old beliefs, and heal deep wounds and resentments. It's a chance to renegotiate relationships, set healthy boundaries and re-assess what makes you—*you*! The authentic you. The one you want to be for the rest of your life.

CHAPTER 10

Why Are Hormones So Darned Important?

WITHOUT A PROPER BALANCE of hormones our bodies cannot function optimally. Hormones impact our mood, weight, bones, skin, memory and, of course, our libido. They also have a huge effect on how we age.

Dr. John W. Rowe, a gerontologist, says how well we age is 70 percent lifestyle choices and 30 percent heredity and environment. That 70 percent gives us incredible power to control how our life evolves. Accepting responsibility for our own quality of life requires that we educate ourselves, understand what a body needs for optimum health and make choices that support us in being vital wise-women.

Your lifestyle choices will have the biggest impact on your metabolism. The word "metabolism" represents all the chemical processes by which cells produce the substances and energy needed to sustain life. As part of metabolism, organic compounds are broken down to provide heat and energy.[39] The health of your metabolism is largely determined by diet, stress and exercise levels, and the toxic chemicals we are exposed to in our food and environment. Our hormones serve as the "juice" that keeps our metabolism running smoothly and regulates the metabolic process by communicating between cells.

By making poor choices, we can quickly age ourselves metabolically and die long before our chronological age says it's time to go. Making choices that don't support a healthy metabolism drag us down a slippery slope into the world of degenerative diseases, such as hypertension, heart disease, obesity, dementia and a whole bevy of conditions we hope to never become familiar with. (Degenerative diseases are not inherited conditions, but those caused by poor eating and lifestyle habits.[40]) It's empowering to know we have some control in this area.

The body is constantly regenerating and undergoing complex chemical reactions in an effort to replenish what has been used. To do that, it needs the proper biochemical building blocks. If you're using too many of these building blocks (through over-exercise, poor diet, high stress, or exposure to toxic chemicals) and not giving your metabolism what it needs to recover (nutrient-rich foods, supplements, lower stress levels, and appropriate exercise), you will become physically unbalanced, and eventually the body will manifest a disease and age more rapidly. Much has been written to suggest that getting "old" is a reflection of diminishing levels of hormones in our bodies and that rebalancing one's hormones can prevent disease and increase vitality.

Doctor Diana Schwarzbein, an endocrinologist, explains in her book *The Schwarzbein Principle II* that there are major and minor hormones. Adrenaline, insulin and cortisol are the three major hormones, and they exert a direct influence on critical functions such as heartbeat, blood pressure, and pH balance. When we have an imbalance of one hormone, it creates a communication breakdown among cells and impedes regeneration. An imbalance or lack of one of these major hormones leads to illness and a shorter life. (Insulin issues lead to diabetes or hypoglycemia; long-term stress leads to dangerous levels of adrenalin and cortisol. These conditions can be lethal.) There is no debate in the medical community on the importance of these hormones and the value of treating their deficiencies.[41]

There is, however, considerable debate in the medical community about the efficacy of replacing the minor hormones, which include progesterone, testosterone, DHEA, human growth hormone (HGH) and the estrogens. While loss of major hormones will likely cause life-threatening conditions, loss of minor hormones will typically cause only low-level discomfort such as fatigue, mood swings, hot flashes, and anxiety. (Of course, they're only low-level when they're happening to someone else!) If you've ever experienced a hot flash or night sweat, you are familiar with the effects of the loss of minor hormones.

Dr. Uzzi Reiss, a Beverly Hills gynecologist, explains:

Hormones are secreted by glands, such as the adrenals, ovaries and thyroid, that are governed by higher centers of the brain. Hormones travel throughout your bloodstream in a communication network that links the higher centers of your brain to the DNA command posts operating in the several hundred trillion cells of your adult body. On the outer and inner membranes of the cells are receptor sites that function like locks on a door. In order to get in and tell the DNA what to do, you need the right key, and hormones are the keys....They travel to specific target cells, unlock the receptor sites, and deliver their biochemical message

You can't turn back the clock. But you can wind it up again.
BONNIE PRUDDEN

for processing. They turn on or turn off specific cellular functions and measure cellular function throughout the system.[42]

So where does your body get the raw material it needs for healthy functioning? *Food!* "You are what you eat" is not just an empty platitude. Nutrients from food give us the biochemical components we need to regenerate our bodies, and our hormones then regulate the chemical reactions. Think about that the next time you're about to dig into greasy foods, sugary snacks or cola drinks. Because of our poor diets, many of us need to take supplements to provide our body with the vitamins and minerals it needs.

Proper levels of hormones are directly tied into our levels of vitality and good health. Hormones also supply our internal organs with the nutrients needed for healthy functioning. Without proper hormone levels, our bodies are unable to operate as intended, and they begin to shut down. In other words, they grow *old*.

Dr. Schwartzbein makes a powerful point by writing,

> *With the loss of a major hormone, you absolutely know that something is medically wrong with you, and if the major hormone is not replaced, you will die rather quickly. With the loss of a minor hormone, you will not feel well, but you are likely to attribute your health to normal aging and not seek medical attention.* **You will eventually die from the loss of a minor hormone, but when you die 10 to 50 years later, who is to know that the minor-hormone loss contributed to your death?**[43] (Emphasis added)

Well, now *you* know! In addition to impacting our overall health and longevity, unbalanced levels of hormones can lead to weight gain, low libido, a compromised skeletal structure, fatigue and memory lapses. Perhaps you already knew that. Or did you forget?

Weighing In

As I moved into my early fifties, I noticed a little extra middle around my middle. My once (almost) flat stomach was becoming downright poochy, to the point where I couldn't even suck it in. My hips had little handles, and every time I sat down, a cascade of flesh (okay, fat) poured over the top of my jeans. I hid it well with loose tops, but I was dismayed when exercise didn't melt it away. I continued to eat healthfully, but somehow I knew that dieting was not going to solve the problem either. Once again, I turned to research.

I don't know how you feel about old age... but in my case I didn't even see it coming. It hit me from the rear.

PHYLLIS DILLER

I learned that this extra layer of fat is healthy at this time in life, and that most of this additional weight accumulates around the belly for a reason! This is not permission to pig-out. We're talking about a mere 5-10 pounds accumulating over a 10-year period.

Our ovaries and adrenal glands secrete a substance called *androstenedione,* which is converted into estrogen by our fat cells. In other words, our belly fat helps us generate estrogen. Women with ample fat reserves typically have less severe hot flashes, stronger bones, and an easier transition overall because their bodies have a built-in way to produce more of the hormones they are lacking.

According to Susan Weed in *New Menopausal Years,* menopausal belly fat does *not* increase your mortality rate. Losing it can actually result in problems with your thyroid, gall bladder, insulin uptake, and even your immune system.[44]

I know, I know. Many of us have spent much of our lives trying to drop those extra pounds, and this can be hard to accept. Our cultural programming is screaming *nooooo!* I'll admit I was distressed to see my middle round out. But when I realized that, once again, my body's wisdom was in charge, I gave myself permission to carry a few extra pounds. The menopausal body needs it. But just for a while.

It is imperative that you continue to exercise, even though it may not eliminate your menopausal belly fat. Both aerobic and weight-bearing exercise will help you develop a strong bone structure and good muscle tone to carry you through life, reducing your susceptibility to injury. Choosing wholesome foods and continuing to exercise, you'll find your weight will usually stabilize.

Through my research, I learned there are some significant drawbacks to carrying too much belly fat *after* we have exited our menopausal years. Abdominal fat is more metabolically active than the fat in other parts of your body. Having too much can tip the scales toward insulin resistance, requiring your body to secrete increasing levels of this hormone to clear sugar from your bloodstream. Having an abundance of this fat may also create an abundance of both androgens and estrogens.[45] In other words, gaining an extra 20 pounds (and keeping it on) later in life diminishes your physical abilities as well as drains your vitality.[46]

Once you're through menopause, your metabolism will usually settle down. Now that I'm coming up on the ten-year mark, I've noticed that my "flotation device" has been significantly minimized.

There are other reasons we tend to put on excess weight during menopause; the primary one is stress. During the years of perimenopause, many women struggle to balance complicated careers, family issues, and personal time—all the while coping with the mood swings and sleeplessness that come with erratic hormones. No wonder we're losing our hair!

When you feel stressed, your body makes a hormone called *cortisol*. During midlife, the fat cells in your abdomen have more receptor sites for cortisol. So, the more stress you have, the more fat cells your body needs to contain the overflow of cortisol. Following the logic, by reducing your stress, you can reduce some of the belly fat.

Ironically, weight gain can also be caused by too much estrogen in relation to progesterone. The research suggests that if you are using supplemental estrogen therapy, it is highly advisable to balance your dosage with natural progesterone (*especially* if you have a uterus).

Common symptoms of too much estrogen are:

Hair loss	Breast tenderness/swelling
Leg cramps	Tummy bloat
Nausea	Recurrent vaginal yeast infections
Depression	

If you are using natural hormone replacement therapy and you gain a lot of weight in a short amount of time or your belly becomes overly bloated, talk to your doctor about retesting your hormone levels and adjusting your protocol. Our needs change as our lives change, and the formulation that helped you last year may not be appropriate for this year.

While menopause does come with a wide range of symptoms, it's *very* important to continue to monitor your health and not ignore messages from your body, thinking, "Oh, it's just menopause." Continue to get regular mammograms (or thermograms), annual Pap smears, blood work and physical exams. Contact your doctor if a symptom continues to bother you for more than a few weeks. Always get a second opinion. Trust your gut, be proactive with your health and give your body the attention it deserves. Remember, sometimes it's more than "just" menopause.

Boning Up

Once you pass 40, "hump day" takes on a whole new meaning… and it's not what you think. (And no, it's not Wednesday.) *Every* day becomes hump day when your bones can no longer support you in standing upright. It's a sad sight to see someone hunched over, trying to make their way through the world with osteoporosis—it is so preventable! It seems that even though we know how to strengthen our bones, the incidence of osteoporosis is increasing.

According to the Center for Science in the Public Interest, one out of six women will fracture a hip. This risk is as high as the risk of breast, uterine, and ovarian cancer combined![47] Almost one-forth of those in nursing homes are there because of a hip fracture. No wonder so many of us harbor a secret fear of falling and breaking a hip or arm. We know this type of injury could limit our quality of life and independence in a nanosecond.

I was very surprised when, at age 54, my bone scan revealed that I had osteopenia. This diagnosis reflects a thinning of the bone and is purported to be a stepping-stone to osteoporosis. Having taken calcium supplements, used bio-identical hormones and been physically active for most of my adult life, I thought my skeletal foundation was strong.

I've since learned that the measurements used to diagnose osteopenia are relative. The standards used to measure bone loss do not take into account our different body types, so a person with a larger bone structure is measured against the same standard as a small-boned woman.

Bone actually consists of both living and non-living materials, and it is constantly being broken down and rebuilt. Early in life, the rate of buildup and absorption are equal, so we have a constant bone mass. Bone growth peaks at around age 30 and begins to slowly decline from there.

Bone loss happens to most of us as we age, but it doesn't *necessarily* mean there is a disease. While it is useful to take steps to strengthen our bones, we don't all need to start taking drugs to do so. Do your homework before you begin any kind of drug therapy, and remember, since most of these drugs are new, there have been few long-term studies done on the effects of these formulations on a woman's overall health. For some women, these drugs are a godsend, but for many of us, simple lifestyle choices, dietary changes, and supplements can help rebuild and maintain a healthy bone structure.

The most common recommendation suggests that a woman should supplement her diet with 1000 milligrams (mg) of calcium and 500 mg of magnesium per day before menopause, and 1200-1500 mg of calcium and 600-750 mg of magnesium per day post menopause. However, nutritionist Dr. Nan Kathryn Fuchs suggests that 2:1 ratio is based on outdated research and provides too much calcium and not enough magnesium. According to Dr. Fuchs (whose conclusions are backed up by other doctors and researchers), this incorrect balance gives us too much calcium, which makes our bones brittle, and too little magnesium, depriving our bones of the flexibility they need to withstand life's daily stresses. On top of that, it might be creating an unhealthy environment within. She writes,

Calcium causes all muscles—including the heart— to contract, while magnesium helps them relax. The

correct mineral balance is particularly important in healthy heart function. You want your heart to both contract and relax. Too many contractions can result in an irregular heartbeat, cause a stroke, or heart attack. Magnesium helps blood pressure become and stay regulated, reduces the formation of plaque in the arteries, and reduces spasms.[48]

She suggests we begin by taking 500 mg *each* of calcium and magnesium, gradually increasing the magnesium to a total of 1000 mg per day, or until you have comfortably loose stools. (Is that ever comfortable?) Many doctors suggest we also supplement our diets with higher doses of vitamin D3 (1000–2000 IU), as it helps strengthen bones and build the immune system. Vitamin D3 should be considered essential for overall health and well-being.[49] You can also help your body manufacture its own vitamin D, which is essential for strong bones, by spending 20 minutes a day in natural sunlight without sunscreen, being careful to avoid the hours between 10 a.m. and 2 p.m., when the sun's rays are strongest and most damaging.

A regular program of weight-bearing exercise, stretching, and balance training can give your body the strength and resiliency to carry you through life. Pilates, yoga, stability ball exercises and Tai Chi are all gentle options to explore.

Remember, do not change or supplement your diet without doing your research and talking with a health-care provider. What works well for one woman may not for another. While we may sometimes wish there was one easy answer for all of us, we are all unique.

Pay attention to the messages you receive from your body, and it will guide you to the best options for *you.*

Am I Losing My Mind?

Can't remember where you parked the car? Forgot your neighbor's name? Standing in the middle of the garage, trying to remember why you went there in the first place?

"Relax," you tell yourself, "brain freezes are normal—the first few hundred times!" When these brain freezes start showing up more often, it's natural to be nervous.

Should you be so concerned? Probably not. Short-term memory loss happens to us all. Forgetting where you put your keys is commonplace. Forgetting what a key is *for* is cause for concern.

Momentary forgetfulness often has more to do with stress, distraction, and feelings of overwhelm than anything physiological. Nonetheless, it can be most exasperating!

Back in my days as a professional speaker, I'd be sailing along, talking about something I knew well, and my mind would suddenly go blank. I would stand there like a deer in the headlights, desperate to remember what I had been talking about. I finally learned to admit what was happening, and my audience always seemed to understand, even offering the missing words.

Can we blame our screwy minds on erratic hormones? Maybe. The jury is still out on whether estrogen levels can affect memory. Some studies using estrogen to improve cognitive abilities found no significant impact. Other research has shown that reproductive hormones are redirected during midlife, stimulating areas of the brain that affect memory. They report that estrogen positively influences language skills, mood, attention, and a number of other functions in addition to memory. [50]

In my own experience, bio-identical estrogen (in tandem with natural progesterone) along with proper

Memory is like an orgasm. It's a lot better if you don't have to fake it.

SEYMORE CRAY

amounts of essential fatty acids did improve my spotty memory. You'll have to experiment to find what works for you. Talk to a doctor who is well versed in menopausal issues, and pay attention to your body's signals.

CHAPTER 11

Natural vs. Synthetic Hormone Replacement

AUTHOR'S NOTE: *As you read about my research and experiences, please understand that I am not medically credentialed; I'm simply a woman who needed answers. Traditional hormone therapies prescribed by the "experts" did not work well for me and I was driven to find alternatives. I have done extensive reading and research into the options that allow me to live more holistically. I am sharing what I learned so that it might give you tools to create a roadmap of your own. I suggest you do your own research and find a medical professional you can discuss options with. The information shared here is in no way intended to be a recommendation for a specific course of action.*

From my years of research, I've come to understand that experts are only experts on what is current knowledge— which is often based on past experience and leaves little room for innovative ideas. Research is often 10 or more years ahead of practice, so when you speak with your doctor, remember that they don't have the time to stay on top of every new study. Share your research with them. If he or she is not open to this, find a doctor who is.

M OST WOMEN EXPERIENCE THEIR most intense menopausal symptoms throughout a 5- to 10-year window of time. These symptoms can be a challenge for many. Thankfully, there are healthful ways to supplement our diminishing hormone levels in order to provide respite to those who are struggling to weather the storm—or who just want a good night's sleep! More than that—hormones keep us vital.

How do we insure that we have balanced levels of these critical hormones available to us in order to keep the body robust and talking to itself?

The major hormones (adrenaline, insulin and cortisol) are regulated primarily by lifestyle choices. If we have run our bodies down to the point where they can no longer maintain a balance, we must take steps to reduce stress, eat more healthfully and exercise adequately. Find a doctor or a nutritionist to help you choose a course of action (and/or supplements) that will help stabilize and balance your metabolism.

We have additional options when it comes to replenishing the minor hormones (progesterone, testosterone, DHEA, human growth hormone [HGH], and the estrogens). There are many controversial articles that have been written on the use of HGH supplements. I suggest you do extensive research and talk to your doctor if you are considering its use.

In the past several decades, millions of women were routinely prescribed synthetic hormones. This protocol was finally questioned by the medical community at large when the Women's Health Initiative (WHI) hormone trial was abruptly halted in July 2002 when it became clear that the women involved, who were using a combination of synthetic estrogen (conjugated equine estrogens, i.e., pregnant mare's urine) and progestin, a synthetic progesterone, were at risk of developing breast cancer, stroke, blood clots and heart disease.

While this realization may have been distressing for many, it seems to be supported by a 2006 study that reported a 7 percent decline in breast cancer rates in 2003 (the year after many women stopped taking synthetic hormones), the largest single drop in breast cancer incidence *ever* reported within a single year.[34] An even more significant decline of 12 percent was found for women between the ages of 50 and 69 diagnosed with estrogen receptor positive breast cancer. Since many breast tumors feed on estrogen, discontinuing supplementation with *synthetic* estrogen may have caused developing tumors to shrink or disappear—and that's good news! Additional reports show the decrease continued into 2004.[35] While these initial years of decline may not tell the whole story, there is agreement in the medical community that, coming as it did on the heels of the WHI study, this correlation is telling. Further research is needed to substantiate the claims.

Ultimately, the results of the WHI study were very useful in determining what *doesn't* work well—*synthetic* hormones that mimic our natural hormones.

Synthetic hormones are problematic not only for the women who take them, but also for the horses that supply them. These hormones are derived from pregnant mares' urine. To collect this urine on a scale that makes it profitable, almost 80,000 pregnant mares must be confined in stalls only as big as the horse itself. For much of their 11-month pregnancy, they are not given much water (don't want to dilute the urine), not allowed to exercise, and may not even be allowed to lie down. After giving birth, they are allowed only a few months with their foals, and then re-impregnated for another round.[36]

Unfortunately, reading and hearing reports on the pros and cons of synthetic hormone replacement therapy without hearing about alternative options leaves many women confused about what to do to alleviate their menopausal symptoms. They often suffer in silence (well… if you've ever seen a woman in menopause, it's not really so silent) or resign themselves to taking a synthetic hormone, all the while worrying about the potential harm they may be doing to their body. This is a sad state of affairs.

Pharmaceutical companies and much of the medical establishment approach menopause like a disease, which it clearly is not. It's a transition. While I have great respect for the work of the drug companies in treating illness and disease, I fear they might be missing the boat on the issue of hormone replacement. Using a drug to supplement your natural hormones may alleviate some symptoms, but often opens a Pandora's Box of potential negative side effects.

My own doctor initially prescribed Estratest, which is a blend of synthetic estrogen and testosterone. While I did feel better in the short term, within several months I began to feel bloated and short of breath, had heart palpitations, gained weight and just felt off. My doctor had few alternatives to offer me, so I went looking for more natural options on my own.

Bio-identical Options

I dove into my research and read numerous articles and studies that introduced me to the world of bio-identical hormones. I am not referring to over-the-counter remedies that profess to have natural ingredients that are precursors to or mimic natural hormones. While some of the over-the-counter remedies may provide some relief, many of them are unregulated, unreliable, and of questionable dosage. This discussion refers to human-identical, plant-based hormone remedies that are prescribed by a doctor and commonly referred to as Bio-identical Hormone Replacement Therapy (BHRT).

Here's what I learned. Bio-identical hormones are not a synthetic version of a natural hormone. Bio-identical means that, while it is not human in origin, it is *chemically identical* to the hormones that your own body produces. Remember, a substance can be natural and not be bio-identical. Horse urine is natural, right?

The basic steroid molecule used in Bio-identical Hormone Replacement Therapy (BHRT) is extracted from either soy or wild yams.* Using a multi-step process, a chemist distills a hormone that is identical to the hormones produced by the human body. These hormones are then mixed into a carrier (pill, gel or cream) by a pharmacist and can be purchased through a compounding pharmacy, that is, a pharmacy that makes prescriptions to order.

BHRT remedies are prescribed for you by a doctor only after your hormone levels have been tested, so the hormone can be specifically compounded to meet your body's needs. It is not a one-dose-fits-all approach, and it requires periodic adjustment based on your lifestyle. What we commonly refer to as "estrogen" is really "estrogen(s)" made up of three separate compounds produced naturally in the body in the following proportions: E1: estrone (10-20%); E2: estradiol (10-20%); and E3: estriol (60-80%).[37] These must be in proper balance to keep our systems functioning well. Two common formulations of BHRT are called Bi-est (formulated with proportionate amounts of E2 and E3) and Tri-est (with proportionate amounts of E1, E2 and E3). The proportions are determined by your individual needs, based on

*Do not be deceived by wild yam creams available over the counter. They contain a precursor to progesterone that is biologically unavailable to humans. Bio-identical estrogen and progesterone must be produced in a laboratory.

hormone testing, in an effort to recapture the ratios your body normally produces. Supplementing with just *one* of the three hormones that make up estrogen (like those used in an estrogen patch) is antithetical to what the body does naturally.

A hormone cream or gel rubbed onto the skin is absorbed directly into the bloodstream and bypasses the liver, thereby causing less stress on that organ. A small dosage can be quite effective, as little is destroyed by the digestive system. Talk to your doctor about whether creams, gels or pills would be best for you.

To complete the protocol, your doctor will usually prescribe natural progesterone, and, if your tests confirm they are low, testosterone or DHEA. Do your own research and confer with a medical professional to ensure you are using these hormones in a proper ratio, based on your own body's needs.

My doctor was willing to consider the research I had done, and together we set up a bio-identical protocol, which we have tweaked over the years as needed.

That was over 10 years ago. Today we have much more information about bio-identical and other natural options available to us. And yet, it concerns me how little some doctors know about bio-identical hormones. Most doctors rely on the pharmaceutical companies for information and solutions; this severely limits our options. As more women ask for effective natural alternatives to synthetic hormones, more doctors are taking the time to educate themselves on their benefits.

Keep Your Eye on the Ball

As you do your research into hormone replacement therapy and the possible alternatives to it, remember to consider the source of the information you read. Many media stories discuss synthetic hormones as if they are the only viable solution for menopausal symptoms. When they mention "estrogen," they are often referring to a pharmaceutical company's synthetic version of the real thing.

Some pharmaceutical companies are concerned about the money they are losing to bio-identical hormones and natural alternatives. They are fighting hard to keep synthetic hormones on the table as a viable option, and they seek to discredit the bio-identical approach by portraying compounding pharmacies as backroom hacks.

Watch for websites and television advertising that appear to be sensitive to woman's menopausal issues but may really be wolves in sheep's clothing, simply there to entice women back into the fold of synthetic hormones. Some pharmaceutical companies are working quietly behind the scenes to persuade Congress to pass laws that will limit women's ability to obtain compounded BHRT, along with many of the natural remedies and supplements many of us now rely on for optimal health. Women must speak up.

Some doctors are now being encouraged to prescribe synthetic hormones to younger menopausal women for short periods of time to see them through the most difficult symptoms. Is this a good approach? Will we have to wait and see if side effects develop? Only time will tell.

Regrettably, there are very few studies being done on the efficacy of bio-identical hormones. Because the pharmaceutical companies are unable to patent a natural substance, they prefer to create a synthetic version of that substance (thus owning the patent *and* the profits). Research seems to follow the money. Then they add to the confusion by claiming that bio-identical hormones are unsafe because there are no double-blind studies to support their safety! It's a classic Catch-22.

And what about our government agencies? The National Institutes of Health? Department of Health and Human Services? By teaming up with the pharmaceutical companies, they were able to find the money for the now defunct WHI study on synthetic hormones. Why aren't they also studying the effects of BHRT? After all, the suggested and potential, albeit mostly untested, benefits of BHRT include minimized heart disease, reduced bone loss, fewer debilitating strokes, retained memory function and a vital population of aging women.

Because so little research has been done, we also don't know the possible negative side effects of BHRT. We simply don't know whether using these bio-identical estrogens will increase rates of heart disease or breast cancer, although anecdotal evidence seems to suggest not. There are also some who believe that BHRT will create dependence, leading your body to become less effective at producing hormones on its own.

Let this information supplement your research, not be the entirety of it. Every individual is different and it's up to each of us to search for our best options. Talk to a doctor or health-care practitioner who is well versed in bio-identical options. There are FDA approved formulations of natural hormones (such as Climara, Prometrium, and Vivelle) that have been proven to have fewer risks than synthetic hormones.

There are many complementary therapies to choose from as well. I found acupuncture very helpful in balancing my energy and reducing the intensity of my menopausal symptoms. It was also a major factor in helping me recover from chronic fatigue.

A doctor or school of naturopathy can also offer hormone-free options to alleviate menopausal symptoms and stimulate the body to produce more hormones on its own.

Herbal infusions of oat straw, nettle or red clover are recommended by Susan Weed, a noted herbalist. She suggests that drinking these infusions daily will help regulate and strengthen the body during this time of transition and smooth out the rough spots naturally.[38]

Whole soy products can also provide our bodies with phytoestrogens (plant-based estrogens) that are reported to help alleviate some of the milder menopausal symptoms. Again, there are advocates for this approach as well as naysayers.

Each of us must decide for ourselves whether or not to include BHRT in our plan to remain a vital, active woman. While I do believe using it has contributed to the overall quality of my life, I would be remiss in recommending it to everyone. I'm not medically credentialed, I don't know whether there might be some negative side effects 15 years down the line, and I appreciate that every woman's history and physiology are unique to her. It behooves each of us to do our research and work closely with a health professional to find the perfect mix of hormones, nutrients, and activities. Be proactive. It's an important step toward making the next 50 your BEST 50!

Always remember that you are absolutely unique. Just like everyone else.

MARGARET MEAD

Sex, Stereotypes and Statistics

RESEARCH SUGGESTS THAT WHAT we believe about how aging affects memory actually affects how well we remember things!

A 2003 study[51] demonstrated that when men and women in late middle age were told that their scores on a memory test would be compared with those of people over 70, they underperformed. Why? It's a phenomenon called the stereotype effect and is seen in other areas of comparison as well. Women who have been told that men are better at math will underperform when taking a math test, believing the stereotype to be true.

In this instance, telling middle-agers they are being compared with the older group sets off the subtle reminder of the link between age and memory loss, and to the extent they *believe* the stereotypical notions about growing old, they will manifest results supporting those beliefs. In effect, we alter our performance to support the stereotype.

It's interesting to note that in another study, where participants took a standard word-recall test, those who

Our life is what our thoughts make it.
MARCUS AURELIUS

were compared to a younger group did as well as that group on the recall. Again, when told they were to be compared to an older group, they faltered. Poor performance was even more notable in men and women who, in a pre-test questionnaire, reported concerns about growing older.

According to Ellen Langer in her book *Mindfulness*:

Most of the arbitrary limits we set on our development in later life are not based on scientific information at all. Our own mental picture of age, based on hundreds of small premature cognitive commitments, will shape the life we lead in our own late adulthood.[52]

We are inundated with negative media images regarding the frailties of the aged; jokes and cartoons abound. Surely you've heard of "senior moments." We laugh, but do you accept these images and jokes as valid, as an inevitable part of growing old? These attitudes and stereotypes seep into our unconscious, and even as early as middle age, they begin to shape our beliefs about what will happen as we get older.

Once again we are reminded that our *beliefs* about aging have a profound impact on *how* we age. We actually have more control over our aging experience than previously thought. Challenging our fears and the limiting beliefs they spawn gives us the opportunity to explore the higher states of being that we seem to crave at this stage of life.

We Amazing Grays have an opportunity to create a *new* stereotype, one that portrays **maturing women as vibrant, healthy, wise, engaged with life, sexually active, spiritually connected, physically fit and alive well past 100**! I could get behind that, couldn't you? No reason we can't give it our best shot—as long as we continue to stimulate our minds, exercise our bodies and explore life.

As we continue to stimulate our minds, we develop new pathways in the brain.[53] We lose brain cells throughout our lives, a process that begins at birth. But once brain cells are lost, we don't necessarily have a deficit for the rest of our lives! Studies have shown that environmental complexity introduced in adulthood can build up the cortex.[54] It seems our brains are capable of new growth and are affected by certain kinds of focused mental functioning.

Regardless of one's age, the brain, like the body, gets lazy if it is not exercised. Without mental stimulation, it's a short trip into the world of depression and anxiety. Here are some things you can do to keep your mind sharp and your spirits high:

The advantage of a bad memory is that one enjoys several times the same good things for the first time.
FRIEDRICH NIETZSCHE

Challenge yourself: You can stimulate your brain to grow new circuitry by occasionally doing everyday things (like brushing your teeth or writing) with your non-dominant hand. By varying your daily routine (such as taking a different route to the grocery store or sleeping on the opposite side of the bed), you can also create new neural pathways. Do crossword puzzles, Sudoku or other mental games. Take classes at a local college. Paint, journal, work with clay or color in a coloring book! Read, sing, act or learn to play a musical instrument. Take on a new career that pushes you to learn something new. Just don't zone out in front of the television.

Nurture social relationships: Being with other people brings all of your senses into play, requiring you to listen, respond to questions and explain your point of view. Look beyond your family. Join Toastmasters, a book or card club, an exercise class, Bible study or meditation group; and have a regular "Girls Night Out" with friends and neighbors.

Exercise: Physical stagnation promotes mental stagnation. Movement is the great elixir of life! When we get plenty of exercise, we keep our hearts strong, which helps the circulatory system feed our brains with the nutrients it needs to perform well.

Be mindful: Most of our mental lapses occur because we're on autopilot. We don't actually forget where we parked the car; we just don't pay attention to where we leave it when we're busy thinking about the grocery list! Stay in this moment, not the next one.

As we struggle to stay on top of the… gaps in our thinking, it helps to know that there is an upside to this process. According to Joan Borysenko,

> *As women, we continue to grow in right-brain function, so that our intuitive capacity, our capacity for empathy, and the ability to grasp the whole, continues as we grow older.… In our brain there is an increased capacity for recognizing pattern and meaning in life.*[55]

We know that our brains are being biologically rewired, so it makes sense that the logical left brain will temporarily slow down to make way for right-brain development.

The next time you can't remember the name of that Italian restaurant you love, relax! Menopausal women may not be winning the jackpots on *Jeopardy*, but we can certainly be content in knowing that the next great adventure is just around the corner.

The word "aerobics" came about when the gym instructors got together and said: If we're going to charge $10 an hour, we can't call it "jumping up and down."

RITA RUDNER

Embracing a New Stereotype

The stereotypical image of a withered, sexless old woman is fading. Emerging to take her place is the picture of the sexually active, vital, wise-woman *we* are creating—you remember: the one that claims that *maturing women are vibrant, healthy, wise, engaged with life, sexually active, spiritually connected, physically fit and alive well past 100!*

We live in a culture that seems to portray sex as a competitive sport where more is better, and if you're not ready to go at a moments notice, you must have some sort of sexual dysfunction. Not so fast. Like many things in life, there seems to be ebb and flow to our sexual cycles as well.

In 2005, *More* magazine conducted a survey of 1,328 readers and offered a revealing look into the sexuality of mature women. It seems that most women in their **forties** are still ripe with passion: Two-thirds say their sex drive is as strong as it was five years ago and find sex more satisfying than it was in their twenties. Slightly over half say the amount of their sexual activity hasn't changed over the last decade.[56]

As women move into their **fifties**, there are some significant shifts: only half of these women still find their sex life more satisfying than in their twenties, and an equal number find they are having less sex than they did ten years ago. Some surprising findings:

Only 41% always have orgasms with their partner
29% only have them sometimes
70% of 50-something women masturbate, and of those, 78% consistently have orgasms
45% use vibrators and sex toys[57]

There's a lot to digest here, so we'll start with this red flag: Why are only 41 percent of women consistently having orgasms with their partners, yet almost two-thirds seem to get the job done quite well by themselves?

Here are a few things to consider: Women in their fifties crave romance and spiritual connectedness in their sexual encounters—but they don't expect them from a vibrator. Sex is a complex connection, and emotional clutter can get in the way of being sexually responsive.

What really turns us on is romance, attention, affection and a slower pace, but many women are reluctant to ask for what they want. Ladies, listen up: you have to teach your partner how to treat you! Our generation has opened the door to intimate communication so we can feel free to talk about our sexuality. Lovingly show your partner what you want. Chances are, they'll respond—and you will too! The most romantic relationships are built on genuine tenderness and respect for each other. By opening up and sharing what is going on for you, and asking your partner to do the same, you create vulnerability and tenderness, the gateway to deep intimacy and connectedness.

Aging men are subject to the effects of diminishing levels of hormones as well. If your partner is constantly tired and having a difficult time staying engaged with life, you might suggest he have his hormone levels assessed by a qualified medical practitioner. It goes beyond sexual virility; it becomes a quality-of-life issue.

One interesting statistic that arose from this survey is that 56 percent of those women on hormone replacement therapy say it had *no* effect on their sex lives. This is another red flag. A full complement of balanced hormones is essential for robust orgasms, so why isn't hormone replacement therapy helping these women? I suspect they used *synthetic* hormone replacement, which for many does not do the job. Synthetic chemicals simply don't provide your body with the physiological connections you need for optimum health and function. While orgasms need not be the goal of every sexual encounter, many of us would rather have them than not. From my own experience, I found that after I balanced my hormones bio-identically, my sexual response kicked back into the realm of *oh... my... goodness.*

The *More* magazine article, like much of the research on adult sexuality, dumped senior sexuality into one age bracket: **60 and beyond**. *Beyond what?* I suspect that as we move into this "beyond" category, our boomer generation will ferret out the differences between sex in our sixties, seventies, eighties and nineties! (Jeez, do we have to do everything?)

The statistics on women in their sixties (and beyond!) showed that 73 percent are in long-term relationships, and of those women...

68% are sexually active, despite the fact that...

71% are having less sex than they did ten years ago, and...

61% would like to up their frequency, except...

41% say their partner isn't willing, which is odd, because...

50% rely on him to initiate sex, but then again...

40% don't have orgasms with said partner. No shock, since...

27% complain about the quality of his erections. Thus...

55% use vibrators.[58] (At least they're resourceful!)

Falling victim to the media messages that surround us, many of us have been conditioned to expect that we will feel bad as we age, that we will lose our strength, vitality and sexuality. It's easy to fall into the trap of believing that this is just how it is to get older. Don't buy into the old stereotype. Remember that the most important sexual organ in your body is your brain. Your experience reflects what you think about most. If you believe you're going to shrivel up and fade away, then you probably will. If you think your aging body can no longer bring you pleasure—it won't. But it doesn't have to be that way! Our bodies want to be healthy and active. If you're not satisfied with the quality of your sex life, do something about it. Now, more than ever, we have options. It's not what life gives you that determines the quality of your existence; it's what you *do* with it that makes all the difference. Nothing is sexier than a woman who exudes confidence and fully inhabits her body. This is your life; live with gusto!

Ouch!

Not many women want to talk about it, but the unfortunate fact is that during the menopausal years, over 60 percent[59] of women experience episodes of painful intercourse. Barely half of these women discuss it with their doctor. This is not something you have to put up with or feel ashamed about. If it hurts, listen to your body! It's trying to communicate with you. There are many causes of painful intercourse; I got to explore these issues firsthand when I stopped taking hormones for a year. I learned that when intercourse becomes too painful to participate, it's time for medical intervention—not withdrawal.

When estrogen levels fall, our bodies can't produce the same amount of lubrication as before. Coupled with thinning vaginal tissue, this makes for a painful sexual experience. The outer one-third of the urethra and the vaginal lining are estrogen sensitive, so a drop in hormones affects their ability to function correctly as well.[60] This is one of the reasons so many of us suffer through recurrent bladder infections in this phase of life, and why they are often remedied with supplemental estrogen.

For some women, especially those in early perimenopause, an over-the-counter vaginal lubricant can alleviate sexual discomfort. Some women use a vitamin E suppository twice a week, which can help the vaginal tissue immensely. Another option is to increase one's intake of phytoestrogens by consuming more fermented soy products (miso, for example) or an herbal infusion.

For those of us in our fifties *and beyond*, it can take a little more than over-the-counter remedies. For me, the physical discomfort was relieved by a prescribed formula of bio-identical estriol (E3) used as a vaginal suppository. Over time, this strengthens and restores elasticity to the vagina, urethra, and surrounding tissue, yet is not absorbed into the bloodstream.

It's wise to also have your hormone levels tested to ensure you have a full complement of all the hormones necessary to support optimal sexual function and vitality. I had my hormone levels retested, and as a result I started using bio-identical hormones again. Within several months of treatment, I found all systems were go: my energy levels were up, my mental clarity increased, sex was enjoyable, and my overall outlook on life improved.

Again, talk to your doctor and do your research. Keep pursuing your options until you find the solution that works for you.

When the Mood Doesn't Strike

Lack of lubrication is the least of our worries when there is no desire in the first place! Is it some kind of cosmic joke that we have the libido rug pulled out from under us just when the kids are gone and we finally don't have to worry about getting pregnant? What is going on here?!

If you'd rather spend the day shopping with your girl-friends than in the bedroom with your lover, you are not alone and there is nothing wrong with you. Low libido is a common side-effect of the change, and I know it well.

For a long time I was not aroused by anyone—and I mean anyone. George Clooney could have climbed into bed with me, and I would have told him to stay on his side and stop hogging the covers. I knew this wasn't how I was *supposed* to feel, so it created a great deal of anxiety and stress. Come to find out, that just made matters worse! Behind hormone imbalance, stress is the second most common cause of low sex drive. The human body is designed to put survival ahead of pleasure (and aren't you glad!), so when stress fires up your adrenal glands, your body shuts down estrogen and testosterone production. These hormones are critical to desire and sexual response.

If you are experiencing a consistently diminished sexual response, don't take it lying down (sorry, couldn't resist). Get yourself into the doctor's office to have your hormone levels assessed. Some women experience low testosterone levels during menopause, and when this is coupled with low levels of estrogen, the juice just goes right out of the girl! Testosterone creams or gels, or supplemental DHEA (a precursor to testosterone), along with appropriate levels of bio-identical estrogen will often kick-start your engine and have you purring once again. Don't be discouraged if you don't notice an immediate improvement. Once you begin using hormonal supplements, it typically takes a couple of months for things to level out physically.

Here's something else to consider: Women who have had pelvic surgeries, such as hysterectomies, or bladder or colon operations, often report a diminished sex drive. When the blood flow and/or nerve function in that area is compromised, it can result in a loss of sexual function.

Even an episiotomy can damage nerves and cause long-term pain, making sex uncomfortable.

Of course, physical reasons for sexual discomfort are only part of the equation. Once you have sorted out the physical issues, you can begin to address the emotional and spiritual aspects of your experience. Rebalancing hormones is not recommended *in lieu of* your inner exploration but rather *as part of* a holistic approach.

It Could Be Something Deeper...

Rather than ingest hormones to quiet the physical symptoms and ignore all the other ramifications of menopause, it's important to remember that our human expression occurs in a broader context. Low libido in menopause is not *necessarily* a physical symptom that needs to be fixed; quite often, it's also a spiritual or emotional issue that needs to be honored. Because the emotional, physical and spiritual aspects of our selves are so intertwined, a shift on one level will usually stir up the others. As we go through a major rewiring of our brains, everything that needs healing starts to surface—especially with your partner. Things that are not right can no longer be shoved under the bed. That mattress can get awfully lumpy, and soon no one wants to lie in the bed!

Watch for hidden resentments, unmet needs and boundaries that are not being honored, and give them a voice. (Remember to use "I" statements when sharing them with a partner.) Without the light of day, these deep-seated feelings can ferment into a smelly pool of anger and bitterness, killing any desire to be close and putting you both in emotional lockdown. After taking steps to assure your hormone levels are balanced:

Take a moment and jot down any feelings or thoughts that might be blocking your sexual response.

Examples:

I feel unappreciated and ignored, which shuts me down emotionally.

I am not attracted to my partner when he criticizes me.

I'm doing 90 percent of the household tasks, even now that he (or she) is retired, and I resent it.

_____

_____

_____

_____

It happened to me. My libido was in the tank. I was getting fat and happy on smoothies. I felt disenfranchised from my marriage. I needed time to sit, be quiet, to write and express myself, but I didn't ask for that, and somehow I started blaming my husband for the fact I wasn't getting what I needed! (How often does *that* happen?) I started to resent his sexual advances and pull away emotionally. It wasn't until I paid attention to what was going on inside of me that I was able to open up and talk to him about it. I had to break through some old conditioning that told me I couldn't ask for what I needed—especially when it didn't include him! Once I recovered my voice and started to communicate my internal experiences, things began to look up.

I was a little mystified by these changes in my sexuality, but then it hit me—this is all part of the plan! As our brains are being physically rewired, our body gives us a time-out so we can rediscover who we want to be when we grow up. Now that our bodies are no longer biologically driven to procreate, that reproductive energy can help us give birth to parts of ourselves we've not known before.

Rather than try to recreate what you had in the past, look to create a new sense of yourself and your sexuality, befitting who you are *now*. As this unfolds, you might be moved to reconnect with your partner in a way that honors you both to the very depths of your souls. It's a different kind of excitement.

Take time to explore your inner musings and discover what you need.

~ Find ways to spend time alone. Go on a retreat or vacation, or just put up a tent in the backyard!

~ Take time to write down your dreams and frustrations. What do you feel is lacking in your life? What is working well? Journal whatever comes up for you.

~ Talk to your partner about what you are going through. Use "I" statements and take full responsibility for your journey. Honor yourself by asking for what you need.

We each have a choice as we move forward into this glorious time of our lives: we can continue to carry our old, familiar baggage, *or* we can dump the trash! Remember, *anything you're willing to tolerate stays in your life*. You get what you settle for. Deal with the cobwebs in the corners, and free yourself to live in the present moment, experiencing life as it unfolds.

Redirect

Some women choose to close the book on their sexuality. They just feel done with that part of life, and that's perfectly okay. Some may be moved to dedicate their lives to a spiritual practice, living monastically or as a missionary. Other women shift into a non-sexual mode for a period of time while their energy is redirected to another passion. We must each honor our own calling. Give yourself permission to listen to the wise-woman within and follow whatever path feels right *to you*. Don't waste your valuable life energy maintaining an old story that has no basis in your new reality (hint: most of them don't).

Understand that this process of sexual evolution is just as much a spiritual awakening as it is a physical transition. Acknowledge your newfound sense of purpose and give an authentic voice to your passions, whatever they may be.

PART THREE

PSYCHOLOGICAL
PERSPECTIVES

Discovering
What's Real

Twenty years from now you will be more
disappointed by the things that you didn't do
than by the ones you did do.
So throw off the bowlines.
Sail away from the safe harbor.
Catch the trade winds in your sails.
Explore. Dream. Discover.

MARK TWAIN

Discovering What's Real

PERHAPS MORE THAN EVER BEFORE IN our lives, maturing women are feeling the need to clear out the physical and emotional residue from the past—and make a fresh start on the next phase of life. Looking within, we ask ourselves:

What do I want to do with the rest of my life? What's really important to me now? Who am I now that I'm no longer a caretaker or breadwinner? What if my parents need help? How can I forgive someone who hurt me? What's stopping me from having the joyful life I desire? Is it too late for me? How can I make a difference? How do I find lasting happiness?

This is the time to revise a familiar childhood question and ask ourselves, "Who do I want to be now that I'm all grown up?" Old dreams and fantasies re-emerge from the shadows of your mind, with new values and intentions guiding you back to them.

Ultimately, this is our chance to open up to the magic and mystery of life, speak up for what we really want, release the weight of judgment and have even more fun in the next chapter of our lives than we did in the last one. We can jump off the treadmill of "self-improvement" and reclaim our authentic self, knowing we are just where we need to be.

Many of us profess to be afraid of failure, or are reluctant to try something new. Upon closer inspection, our fears may reflect something much deeper. Author Marianne Williamson offers us a gentle reminder.

*Our greatest fear is not that we are inadequate. Our deepest fear is that we are powerful beyond measure. It is our light, not our darkness, that most frightens us. We ask ourselves, Who am I to be this brilliant, gorgeous, talented and fabulous? Actually, who are you **not** to be?… As we let our own light shine, we unconsciously give other people permission to do the same. As we are liberated from our own fear, our presence automatically liberates others.*

It's your life… how do you want to live it?

CHAPTER 13

A Weight Is Lifted

I NITIALLY, I WAS SO distracted by the physical symptoms of menopause that I didn't pay close attention to all the psychological drama and upheaval that was simmering inside. The collection of stories I carried around in my head about the past and my nagging fears about the future were getting heavier by the day and suffocating my ability to live my life in the *now*. (Sound familiar?)

To continue my journey and prepare myself for what's next, I needed to lighten my load, both physically and emotionally. I decided to clean house, take out the garbage, adopt new perspectives and establish new routines. I wanted to live my life unencumbered by the past. I wanted a fresh start, an opportunity to make myself over as the person I choose to be.

By cleaning out my emotional backpack (suitcase?) and letting go of old stuff, I was able to stand tall, unrestricted by past wounds and future expectations, and look my real possibilities in the eye.

Where to begin?

Often people attempt to live their lives backwards: they try to have more things, or more money, in order to do more of what they want so that they will be happier. The way it actually works is the reverse. You must first be who you really are, then, do what you need to do, in order to have what you want.

MARGARET YOUNG

First, Clean House

Yes, literally! How much stuff are you dragging around that simply weighs you down? For many of us, there comes a time when we feel the urge to divest ourselves of the weight of our material possessions, yet we feel reluctant to let go, believing that we *need* all this stuff to help keep our memories alive. You might find that as you let go of the stuff in your life, those precious memories will remain intact and you will not need a physical memento to conjure up the image. Those memories are part of the very fabric of your life, and can be relived anytime you choose.

So, go ahead and clean out your closets, your dresser drawers, the garage, attic, basement or storage space. By clearing out old stuff you create a clean, fresh space for something new to appear—even if it's just a clean, fresh, empty space! This is not about downsizing, which is an "outside-in" process of restriction, limitation and cutting back while still trying to keep the past alive. Divesting yourself of goods is an "inside-out" process that stems from a personal need for more freedom, spaciousness, and a new beginning.

Buy a book on getting yourself organized or hire a professional organizer who can guide you to make wise choices on what to let go of, what to keep, and where to put it. Clear the clutter from your life.

To make it simple, create three piles and label them:

Keep   Give Away   Toss

Pull everything out of your closet and put back only the garments that fit and that you've actually worn in the past year (not including party clothes). Be brutal. Do you really need 14 white cotton tops? Or 10 pairs of tattered sweatpants? Put them in one of your piles. If you find this process difficult, invite a good friend to come over and support you in letting go of what no longer suits you. If she's a really good friend, she will tell you that the clingy angora sweater you covet is a sacrilege, and that the box-pleated skirt you are hoping will come back in style will never flatter you again, even if it does make a comeback. Toss out your elastically challenged panties and bras and go buy new undergarments—that fit you! Polish your shoes, and send those that are uncomfortable to one of your piles.

Next, sort through the various storage spaces in your home. Go ahead, give away that candleholder you had always hoped to find a use for. Let it all go—mismatched dishes, glassware you'll never use again, knickknacks from the 1980s. Toss those throw pillows that match the sofa you gave away five years ago and acknowledge the truth—you will never get them re-covered. Have a yard sale, give things to your kids, or call a charity to come and pick up your excess baggage. Simplify! You might be pleasantly surprised at how little you actually need around you to be happy.

It is so freeing to be unencumbered by a lifetime of stuff that clutters your life and keeps you anchored in the past. Certainly you'll want to keep things that have special meaning to you, but display them in a way that you can enjoy them. What use are they sitting in a box somewhere?

For many of us, the first half of life was spent accu-mulating all the material possessions that we believed would make us happy. We got the house. (Yippee!) We bought the car we wanted. (Yea!) A new sofa. (Oh, that's nice.) Another dress. (Ho-hum.) Sooner or later, we realize that the "happiness" we felt from these things was temporary at best. Consequentially, the second half of life is often about letting go of excess stuff because we now understand that it's not the source of happiness. These possessions begin to own us, rather than the other way around.

It's hard to convince someone who has not achieved a certain degree of financial success that it doesn't really bring true satisfaction. Sure, money buys you choices, but rarely can it buy happiness. Looking outside ourselves for happiness simply sends us on a never-ending cycle of *more, better, different.* It seems that in this country, many of us have to first experience material success in order to understand that real happiness lies beyond it.

It slowly begins to dawn on us that what we've been looking for is *how we think we will feel when we have all the stuff we want.* Freedom comes from knowing that the feeling comes not from anything we can sleep in, sit on, or wear, but from living each moment fully present, regardless of what's around us.

That could keep you happy for a looong time. (We'll explore how in Part Four.)

Second, Clean House

Now it's time to do for your insides what you did for your home—clean up and clear out.

Pay attention to the issues and emotions that arise to be healed during your monthly cycles and/or hot flashes. While they might be difficult to face, the real damage comes from hanging on to them. If you repeatedly throw garbage into a stream, eventually the water stops flowing, and the stench of pollution makes spending time there unbearable. By allowing your mental and emotional garbage to back up and pollute your psyche, you continually recreate distress in your body. Eventually, your body will manifest a symptom of this *dis*ease: hypertension, heart disease, cancer, high cholesterol, etc. The only way

When the mind is full of memories and preoccupied by the future, it misses the freshness of the present moment. In this way, we fail to recognize the luminous simplicity of mind that is always present behind the veils of thought.

MATTHIEU RICARD

to get the stream to flow freely again is to remove the garbage.

Much of this garbage is created by our negative thinking and limiting beliefs. These thoughts produce our feelings. Our error is in believing that because we *feel* something we have to *do* something. *I feel anxious so I need to make a change. I feel angry so I need to express it. I feel unhappy so I need to leave my partner.*

Rather than take such drastic measures, I found it more useful to just pay attention and stay with the feeling. Sitting still, I observed how the sensation moved through my body and noticed any thoughts that came up. I didn't *believe* the thought, I just observed it. I find that when I pay attention and just watch, the urgency to do something often dissipates. Try it for yourself the next time you have an urgent need to do or say something. Just breathe, observe, and watch what happens.

By paying attention, most of us will learn to differentiate between the issues of a lifetime surfacing to be healed, and those that are hormonally induced. That's why it is useful to have your hormone levels tested periodically and, if necessary, begin to replenish them healthfully. If issues keep arising once the hormones are balanced, then you know it's time to do some internal work.

Using this process, you will soon be able to identify the difference between the musings of your spirit calling you to higher ground and the tiresome patterns of your conditioning using your hormonal imbalance to run a scam.

Even if you've done some inner work and gained a deeper perspective on what life is truly all about, even if you've worked on your childhood wounds, even if you've learned to let go of the people and events that used to drive you nuts… it's time to clear out the emotional stragglers. I'm talking about those unhealed parts of ourselves

Some people are always grumbling because roses have thorns. I am thankful that thorns have roses.

ALLOPHONES KARR

that show up over and over and continue to draw negativity and drama into our lives; the thoughts and feelings that keep us from truly enjoying life. This kind of baggage can make us feel much older than our chronological years.

For some of us, painful experiences in the past continue to wreak havoc with our sense of well-being. Perhaps something or someone harmed you in a way that seems unforgivable. You feel like you can't let it go. A part of you doesn't *want* to let it go. These feelings and thoughts become very familiar, predictable patterns of anger and upset.

Holding on to these wounds can keep you from recreating a vital, meaningful new beginning for yourself, and ultimately harms you more than the original experiences. You continue to relive the events over and over again, flooding your body with stress hormones that elevate your heart rate and blood pressure. When we tenaciously hang on to painful memories and refuse to let them go, we live in an ongoing state of stress, which takes its toll on our minds and bodies and ultimately ages us more quickly.

Did you know that our brains do not distinguish between an experience that's really happening and one that we imagine or remember? That's how powerful our thoughts really are! Our bodies physiologically respond in the same way to a real experience as to an imagined or remembered one. We can actually relive traumatic experiences just by calling up the memory. We cry, tremble, and feel as helpless as the day they actually occurred. The same can happen when we worry about something that may never take place! Why put yourself through this again and again?

The next time your stress and misery are triggered by a memory, ask yourself how old you feel. Don't over-think it; a number will usually come to mind. This is most likely the age you were when the original wounding took place.

If it isn't already evident to you, there is no need to try and figure out what happened all those years ago. These wounds simply need attention and compassion, someone to listen to them. You can be that person for yourself, odd as that might sound. We all have a compassionate wise-woman inside who knows exactly what to do or say. Center yourself in her wisdom and ask the wounded person within what she needs. Then listen, and help her.

Honoring your wounds in this way can be the first step toward healing. You might need to slow down and take some time for yourself. Perhaps you need to set healthy boundaries or confront a person who is treating you poorly. Maybe you need to pull the cork out of your creativity. It could be time to let go of all the busyness and shoulds in your life and book a vacation or a retreat. Ultimately, you have to reassure that hurt part of yourself that you will not allow her to be hurt, ignored or abused any longer.

Sometimes… it takes more.

Forgiveness

Hanging on to anger and resentment is like swallowing poison and hoping someone else will die.

Throughout our lives we encounter situations that can cause us to feel slighted, taken advantage of, ignored or betrayed. Usually with time, and perhaps a little help, we are able to let go of the hurt or resentment and move on. Sometimes not. When we don't, these grievances chew up our insides and hold our hearts hostage, leaving us unable to fully open up to the love and acceptance we deeply desire. It would seem that forgiveness is a gift you give your*self*.

Forgiveness does not mean sweeping things under the rug, stuffing your feelings or pretending there is

To be angry is to let others' mistakes punish yourself. To forgive others is to be good to yourself.
MASTER CHENG YEN

nothing wrong. You don't just forget about it. It doesn't even require that you have contact with the offender. It's all about changing your relationship to the experience so it doesn't tie up your energy. Ultimately, through forgiveness, one gives up the wish that the past could have been different.

Forgiveness is a skill, so it's something we can learn. There are many techniques that can help facilitate the healing process, but the first and most important part is sincere willingness. We must be willing to acknowledge our feelings, explore our inner dialogue around the issue, and let the past fade into the past.

Carrying around this baggage can make us feel much older than our chronological years. Look inside yourself and uncover any wounds that are still festering. Ask yourself, "Do I really want to carry this burden with me into the next half of my life, or am I willing to heal and let it go?" Picturing your future without all the hurt from the past may help you find the willingness to heal in the present.

For many women, these unhealed wounds stem from some form of abuse. Data reported in 2005 on the Rape, Abuse and Incest National Network website states that every two and a half minutes, someone in America is sexually assaulted.[61] One in six American women are victims of sexual assault, and one in three were sexually abused as children. The problem may be even more extensive, as a huge percentage of assaults are never reported.

Sadly, these numbers suggest that many women reading this very book have experienced abuse in their lives. This trauma can be difficult to heal. If these abuses happened when we were children, we didn't have the power to stop them, nor the wisdom to know it wasn't our fault. Even adult women who have been raped or abused struggle with the feeling that somehow they must have been at fault. Many of us carry this unhealed trauma throughout our adult lives, reliving the helplessness, shame, anger and pain over and over again. In order to open our hearts to all the grace and beauty that life can offer, we need to free ourselves from the confines of past traumas. We need to forgive so that we can move on.

I know the truth of this firsthand. My own trauma came at the hands of my alcoholic father. When I was a child I was emotionally and physically abused, and as a pre-teen, exploited sexually. For much of my adult life, this childhood abuse defined me. I was angry and resentful. I pushed people away from the deepest parts of me. I felt shame. I felt like a victim. Eventually, through the help of a good therapist and my spiritual practice, I was able to put the experience in perspective and slowly begin to forgive.

For many of us, a very young aspect of ourselves was wounded. Forgiveness, being an inside job, needs to come from that centered, loving part of yourself that can honor the pain and suffering of this younger part without identifying with it, without becoming it. It is from this compassionate center that healing can begin.

Sometimes, it's useful to tell your story to a tender-hearted witness who's willing to just listen, offering comfort and presence but no advice. Telling your story and being listened to actually changes your energetic patterns and promotes healing.

Journaling can also be a powerful tool in the healing process. Write down what happened and how you feel about it. Wait a couple of days to read what you wrote. This can help you see things in a new light and release old perspectives. Writing about your experience with your non-dominant hand can also help you bypass your logical left brain and aid you in accessing the emotional core of your wound.

If you feel strong enough, put yourself in the shoes of the offender. What might they have been thinking or feeling? What might have happened in their life that made them say or do whatever they did? Perhaps your feelings will soften when you understand the offender's experience.

The goal of forgiveness is not to condone another's actions but to help you to shift into compassion and understanding, so that you are left whole and healed. Forgiveness is like a soothing balm to the soul; it takes the sting out of the wound.

This can be a process that unfolds gradually. I "kind of" forgave my father, but the ability to completely let go of my trauma eluded me. It wasn't until I was in my early fifties and my dad was dying from cancer that I was able to forgive completely. Seeing him so weak and helpless and afraid, I was surprised to also see his innocence. From a centered place, I was flooded with compassion for how he had suffered most of his life. I knew he had been knocked around as a child, had lost his mother suddenly, and went through horrific experiences as a soldier in World War II. He had no one to talk to about the atrocities he witnessed and had therefore internalized his anger and grief. Alcohol was his primary source of relief, but once he was liquored up, his rage was unleashed. While this knowledge doesn't excuse or condone his behavior, it helped me understand it.

As he lay dying, I tried to ease his physical and emotional pain, administering both morphine and forgiveness. I held his hand. I told him that while I forgave him and I believed God forgave him, he needed to forgive himself. He was so afraid that he was going to hell because of the way he had behaved. I suggested he had already been through hell, and that where he was going he would experience more love than he ever thought possible. I jokingly asked him to send me a sign from the other side to let me know he made it.

He died in his living room on a Thursday afternoon. My mother, sister, husband and I were present. I was relieved to see him released from pain, and I was very sad that he had lived such a tortured existence.

After we spent time grieving, we all needed to sleep. My husband and I spent the night across town at my aunt's home; my sister stayed with my mother.

About 6:30 the following morning, I was awakened— not *by* anything, just awakened—and I was moved to walk into the living room. I pulled back the curtains and gasped... before me was one of the most spectacular sunrises I had ever seen. The sky over the blue-gray mountains was streaked an intense rosy pink, and the clouds were vibrant with the colors of ripe peaches and lemons. Tears filled my eyes, and I had no doubt that my dad was letting me know—*Everything Is All Right.*

I called my sister about 9:00 that morning to check in and see how she and Mom had slept. She chortled, "I slept fine until Mom woke me up at 6:30 to look at the sunrise." All three of us were awed by the same sunrise at the same time from two different locations!

While I don't believe my dad created the sunrise, I do believe it was the energy of his presence that inspired all three of us to awaken at the same time to partake of its beauty. His final act created for us a moment of true grace.

It was the healing salve of compassion that finally allowed me to completely forgive my dad. A huge weight had been lifted from my shoulders. I felt myself grow stronger, able to stand tall and look the world straight in the eye. As a child I was a victim. As an adult, I only remain a victim if I allow the abuse to play over and over in my mind or refuse to heal. It's a choice we all have.

Are you willing to forgive, or do you want to take it to your grave? The most difficult people in our lives are often our best opportunities for growth. Look at your own life. Are you holding anger or resentment that keeps you from feeling joyful? Present? Available for your life now?

~ Are you willing to forgive someone who has wronged you?

~ If not, what do you gain by holding on to the pain and suffering? There is always a payoff. What is it for you?

~ Are you willing to let that anger and resentment go, and see if there might be something better for you on the other side of your pain?

~ Can you identify the good that might have come from the situation—something you learned?

~ Give yourself permission to forgive. (Not condone. Just forgive.) Do it for yourself.

~ Choose one of the techniques discussed previously, or any other option that works for you. Have a conversation with the wounded person inside. Journal your feelings and become a tenderhearted witness to your own pain. What might you say to a good friend who was communicating this pain to you? Can you be as compassionate with yourself?

~ If you need to, find a compassionate person to serve as a tenderhearted witness to hear your story, one last time.

Finally, begin to let it go. A process I've found very useful is to visualize putting the wounding experience and all its attending feelings into the basket of a hot-air balloon. Mentally cut the ropes, one by one, and allow the balloon to float away. Watch it until you can no longer see it. Take a deep breath and feel the open space inside your heart. Fill it with love and compassion for yourself.

The process of forgiveness takes as long as it takes. Be gentle with yourself, and do not allow the voices of your conditioning to use your past experience to continually beat you up. When you hear messages like, *"You should have stopped it. It's your fault. Shame on you. I can't believe you're still upset over what happened so long ago,"* know that this is the voice of your conditioning and is not true. Simply acknowledge the voice—"uh-huh"—and be gentle with yourself. Trying to resist and argue with the voices will only give them more power. The wise-woman within knows it's not true. That's all that matters.

Studies have demonstrated that women who experienced physical or sexual abuse as children are much more likely to experience exaggerated responses to stress as adults and suffer more depression, anxiety and emotional disorders.[62] Please do not be reluctant to seek professional help with these issues if you feel overwhelmed or depressed. Asking for help is a sign of strength and will serve you well in dropping the poison that has brought you so much pain and suffering.

To move forward, we need to let go of the past and live fully in the present. Life is precious and worth living unencumbered.

When we are unable to find tranquility within ourselves, it is useless to seek it elsewhere.

FRANCOIS DE LA ROCHEFOUCAULD

∝

Life is short,
Break the rules,
Forgive quickly,
Kiss slowly,
Love truly,
Laugh uncontrollably,
And never regret anything that made you smile.

UNKNOWN

CHAPTER 14

Boomer Angst

W HAT GOES AROUND COMES around. Once we finally come to appreciate that we are accountable for our own happiness and peace of mind, many of us discover that everything that doesn't support our newfound sense of self will surface once again to be healed. Relationships that have haunted, harmed or humored us present themselves to be embraced in a way that honors the grown-up person we've become. We get to look at the part we play in the drama, and decide whether we'd rather be right… or happy. We have an opportunity to choose the quality of relationships we wish to participate in and *be* the person we've been looking for.

And darn it if it doesn't always start right in your own backyard!

So, your Prince (or Princess) Charming doesn't look quite as charming as he (or she) once did? Don't despair. Aging with a partner can be a gift.

One of the most useful books I've ever read on relationships is *Getting the Love You Want* by Harville

Hendrix.[63] According to Hendrix, we magnetically attract partners who mirror our issues, which creates the opportunity for us to work through them. However, if we don't take these opportunities to heal ourselves, we will continue to recreate the same dance with a different partner, and soon find ourselves experiencing the same misery that made us want to leave our previous relationship. And so it comes boomeranging back to us, over and over again, until we finally breathe a fresh breath of conscious awareness into the pattern.

It doesn't much signify whom one marries, for one is sure to find out the next morning that it was someone else.
SAMUEL ROGERS

In this way, intimate relationships can be our greatest opportunities to heal ourselves. Hendrix suggests that in the security of partnership, all the unloved and disowned parts of ourselves—the parts that need to be embraced and attended to—can finally bubble up to the surface to be healed. Because we tend to attract those with our same level of woundedness, our partner and closest friends can mirror our deepest issues. For example, if you don't love yourself, you'll probably attract someone else who doesn't like themselves much either. It seems like some kind of joke, doesn't it? You're both looking to get from the other what neither of you has in the first place. Ultimately, by not loving yourself, you will forever be looking for someone else to do it for you.

Hopefully, by now, most of us know *that* doesn't work!

The good news is that people are innately self-healing. The inner wisdom we each possess attracts to us individuals and circumstances that will trigger our unhealed wounds and eventually push us (often kicking, screaming and blaming) into looking within and embracing those parts of ourselves that need attention. We are each given multiple opportunities to heal the wounds and negative beliefs that keep love at arms length.

If you...	You will attract someone with...
Fear abandonment	Commitment or infidelity issues
Fear intimacy	Insecurity, neediness
Are frugal, money = security	Big spending habits, money = fun
Are spontaneous	A need to plan
Fear being controlled	A need to control

And vice versa.

These opportunities are often quite challenging, and they require a willingness to own our pain and not blame others. Unfortunately, many of us allow our conditioned egos to make decisions, and with the ego in charge, we're "outta there", running way from our pain rather than staying put and healing our wounds. Inevitably, we find ourselves in the same relationship with a different person.

A key lesson in my life has been to recognize that "wherever I go, there I am." I've learned that no matter where I go, no matter whom I partner with, I carry my story with me. The one thing common to all the drama in my life is *me*!

We don't see things as they are; we see them as we are.
ANAIS NIN

I noticed that one of my core issues, fear of abandonment, seemed to travel with me regardless of who joined me in relationship. In essence, I became like a magnet, polarized to attract my opposite. Because I feared abandonment, I found myself in relationship with men who were emotionally unavailable, unwilling to commit or unfaithful—and I kept blaming them! This pattern continued until I accepted accountability to heal myself.

It was only through self-awareness that I began to understand that I actually abandon my *self* by trying to live up to others' expectations of who I should be, even if it's contrary to who I actually am.

The only things that ever stood between me and a loving, fulfilling relationship with another person were the unloved and unhealed parts of myself. Perhaps that might also be true for you? Until I looked within, I was on an endless (and unsuccessful) search for other people to make me feel safe and loved. It took me several tries, looking for that magical someone, before I realized that no one *else* could do that for me.

Deep down, we all seem to share a basic human need to simply be loved and accepted for who we are. Most of us, however, are unaware to what extent these unmet needs have been controlling our lives!

We want to conform, achieve, follow the rules and do it right so that we will be seen and loved. Instead of loving and accepting ourselves, we look for someone else to do it for us. By and large, many of us will do whatever it takes to get acceptance and approval from others, selling ourselves out in the process.

Have you ever worn or done something that made you feel uncomfortable and "not me" in an effort to please someone else? Donned slinky black teddies that showcased your… cellulite? Stayed late even though you had to get up early? Worn unnaturally pointy shoes with heels so high that your foot pain drowned out the social event around you?

Whether in response to a partner, a colleague, or societal pressures, women have learned to barter their authentic selves for external validation. We trade our time, energy, and resources for approval, selling ourselves short in the process and losing our grasp on our authenticity.

Author Martha Beck says,

Pleasing others is like sex: When we do it because we really want to, it's a wonderfully life-affirming way to strengthen a relationship, but when it's motivated by obligation, powerlessness, or calculated advantage, it's the very definition of degrading. The key to an authentic emotional life, like the key to an authentic sex life, is to follow your real desires.[64]

Once we stop looking outside ourselves for validation, we can honor and embrace the person we genuinely are and be present to ourselves. Our "abandonment magnet" (as an example) will lose its polarization and we will no longer attract partners with related issues. It's the law of attraction at work for our higher good!

Perhaps the purpose of a good relationship is to press our hot buttons until we no longer allow them to set us off!

When I attended to and healed my own wounds, I ended up receiving what I'd been searching for all along—forgiveness, love and acceptance *from myself*. It seems I was wasting my energy trying to get other people to change and give me what I thought I needed to be happy. I erroneously believed that *I'd* feel better if *they* were different.

Woman, was I *wrong*.

It's often easier to blame the other person. In truth, an ego in search of evidence will always find it. It's as if we have blinders on and can see only those things that support our case. Yes, we get to be "right," but that's *all* we get to be.

Freedom comes when we each accept responsibility for our own life. We are not victims. I often remind myself that every time I point a finger at another, there are three fingers pointing right back at me. Unless the other person is downright abusive, we can all benefit from staying

When we love a person, we accept him or her exactly as is: the lovely with the unlovely, the strong with the fearful, the true mixed in with the facade, and of course, the only way we can do it is by accepting ourselves that way.
FRED ROGERS

engaged in partnership and tending our own side of the street. It's been said that it takes just one person to change a relationship, and the person you see in the mirror is the only one you have any control over. It took me a looooong time to get that. Sometimes, things of great importance tend to sink in slowly.

By now it should be evident that a special someone who will finally make you feel totally loved and accepted does not exist "out there." You will forever be disappointed in the people you fervently believe to be "the one" who will love and accept you as you are. Others come with their own baggage. It is a sign of maturity when we finally accept that we must do it *for ourselves*. (Isn't it a relief to know that we *get* to do it for ourselves?)

The most important person to completely love and accept you as you are is the one looking back at you from the mirror. How freeing it is when you're no longer dependent on someone else for your sense of self-worth! The irony is that when we truly love and accept ourselves for who we are, we attract others who then validate that message. Isn't life grand?

When we embrace this truth, we stop being victims of external events, blaming others, waiting and hoping things will change, and we start being accountable for our own life experience. It's not about what happens to us, but how we experience what happens to us. Once we can own our part, find ways to forgive and get on with our lives, we live with a fresh perspective of self-reliance and vitality.

Once you have taken steps to become the person you want to be with, you can then begin to draw a loving partnership to you.

You are only young once, but you can stay immature indefinitely.
OGDEN NASH

Think about the *qualities* you would like to have in a partnership. (Trust, fun, passion, etc.)

~ Jot them down.

_____

_____

_____

_____

~ See yourself in that partnership; feel the emotions.

~ Assure yourself that you are self-responsible, worthy and willing to have what you want, and write down several statements affirming that:

Examples:

I deserve to be in a loving relationship with a person who honors all of who I am and isn't afraid to show it.

I love my life and am open to experiencing passion and intimacy.

I am willing to acknowledge my wounds and not blame my partner for causing them.

I am whole and happy unto myself, and my relationships support that.

I am happy and complete unto myself whether I am in an intimate relationship or not.

Continue to be the person you'd like to find. Integrate the qualities on your list into your own life. Expect to receive what you order, and do not listen to the inner voices who proclaim otherwise! Being happy and satisfied with your own life often attracts people and experiences that just might surprise and delight you.

"The most exciting, challenging and significant relationship of all is the one you have with yourself," says Carrie in her role as narrator. *"And if you find someone to love the you you love,"* she concludes, *"well, that's just fabulous."*

SARAH JESSICA PARKER
AS CARRIE BRADSHAW

The "Sandwich Generation"

Many women in midlife find themselves squeezed between their responsibilities to their own children and family and those to an aging parent or relative. (Gives a whole new meaning to feeling like a piece of meat, doesn't it?)

Our society gives lots of kudos to women who take on this heroic effort, often at the expense of their own mental and physical health and spiritual well-being. This programming runs deep. We all want to be seen as good daughters, mothers and wives, and to garner the love and approval that comes from meeting these standards. This is another example of how we strive to be the "right person," worthy of love and approval.

Unfortunately, these demands often arise just at the time when women are being physically rewired to move beyond nurturing and taking care of others. We are looking to explore opportunities, follow our passions and try new things. Many of us are examining ways to answer deep spiritual callings and honor the yearnings of our souls. Suddenly, the string on our balloon of possibilities is pulled short, strangling any notion of flying free.

Our deep-seated need to nourish and tend to others can lead women to ignore their own needs. Keeping the peace and sacrificing self are often necessary to maintain a sense of security in a family. While we are biologically prodded and socially rewarded for putting others' needs before our own, subtle resentments can begin to build over time. If not acknowledged, they can wreak havoc with our overall health.[65]

There are no easy solutions, but there are solutions.

As the oldest daughter, I carried within me the belief that I would be the one to take care of my mother, if and when she needed it. As it turned out, one of my younger brothers and his wife willingly stepped up to the plate, inviting her to live with them. Another brother and his family live nearby and participate by taking her to church or on outings. After a few pangs of guilt—and a heavy dose of "supposed to"—I now appreciate the wisdom in this arrangement, and everyone is satisfied.

Women who feel compelled to take on such huge family responsibilities must take a really deep look within and be brutally honest with themselves about their motives for doing so. There are very few things in life that we *have* to do (contrary to what your conditioning might tell you). We always have a choice, and every choice carries consequences. Taking one road means that you can't take the other. We must each look at the big picture before we decide.

If you're faced with the possibility of caring for an elderly or infirm relative, you might consider some questions and allow yourself to open up to possibilities.

Who says you must be the responsible one?

I encourage you to challenge your (unconscious) belief that says you must take on the role of caretaker. What about your siblings and relatives? Can they help in some way? At the risk of upsetting the family applecart, insist that others put in their fair share, whether it be money, time or resources. Just because they are men, or younger, or busier than you does not mean they can't cook an occasional meal, wield a vacuum cleaner or make a trip to the grocery store. If others are unable to help directly, perhaps they could make a financial contribution. In many cases, there are government resources available to help shoulder the burden. Contact an elder hotline for information on what is available in your area.

Are you the "only one" able to take care of this person?

Be careful how you answer that. We sometimes like to believe that nobody can do it better—thereby making ourselves indispensable and assuring ourselves the love and approval of others. Sometimes, our conditioning will try and convince us that we are the only ones who can do it right. Be wary when your internal voices start to throw words like that at you.

What are you trying to prove? Whose love are you trying to win?

Some people believe that taking care of a parent will finally get them the love and attention they missed as a child. Maybe, if you just do the right thing, they will see what a good person you are and finally give you the love you deserve. Sadly, things rarely work out that way. That kind of emotional hole can never be filled by anyone *else* once we are beyond our childhood years. Are you willing to sacrifice your own family and peace of mind on a long shot? Ultimately, the love we are searching for out there can only be given to oneself, by oneself. Love yourself enough to be honest.

How will you take care of yourself if you take on the care of another person?

If you're going to accept additional responsibilities, make a contract with yourself to continue doing the things that keep you healthy. Schedule them in! Take an exercise class, a yoga class, a long walk alone, or go to a movie. Do these things for the same reason you put on your own oxygen mask first if your airplane loses pressure: you're no good to anyone if you don't take care of yourself.

Can your immediate family take on more responsibilities at home?

Learn to set healthy boundaries and stand up for your own needs. Having your kids and/or partner help with more of the cooking, shopping and cleaning can help enormously. Making them accountable for their own laundry can free up your time so you can devote it to someone who needs you more.

Are you doing it from a sense of obligation or because you truly want to? How do you know?

Giving help and assistance to someone in need can be very rewarding and energizing—*if* that assistance comes from a centered and loving place within you. Is that how you feel? (It's the difference between service and servitude.) If not, perhaps there is something below the surface that needs addressing. Pay attention. Are you resentful? Are you getting enough sleep? Exercise? How is your blood pressure? Your heart? Your overall health? Have you marginalized your spiritual practices, such as church services or meditation? These are warning signs that you're overextending yourself; listen to these messages. Take steps to ensure you live the life you *choose*, not one that has been dictated by societal expectations.

That said, sometimes circumstances are beyond our control, and we have to step up to the plate and gracefully *choose* the life we *have*. It's the difference between dropping your shoulders and accepting the load like a victim, or viewing it from a spiritual perspective and surrendering to life's bigger plan. It's another opportunity to watch your resistance, let it go, accept what is and live life mindfully. Intention is powerful, but the outcome doesn't always look like you might imagine.

To have courage for whatever comes in life—everything lies in that.

SAINT TERESA OF AVILA

Experiment with Yes!

As we get older, many of us get quite comfortable in our ways. It's easy to stay in the comfort zone that has become our life. The habit of saying *no* grows stronger—a warning that we are taking another step down that slippery slope of getting *old*. But take heart: with a little awareness and practice, that resistance can be replaced with receptivity to whatever is happening in the present moment.

I recently tried a little experiment. For one week I decided to say *yes* to whatever life offered me. A friend called and wanted to meet for lunch. I was very busy with my writing and I really wanted to stay home, but in keeping with my experiment I said *yes*. Turns out she couldn't make it and canceled. I got to stay home and write. Hmmm.

My daughter called to ask if my granddaughter could stay with us for a week while she took a summer "girl-friends" vacation. As much as I adore my granddaughter, my inner voices said, "The timing is bad, it's a whole week, your life will be put on hold, you won't be able to write while she is here, yada, yada, yada." Keeping my commit-ment to myself, I said *yes*, and of course I loved every minute of her visit.

Being with a toddler is a wonderful opportunity to stay in the present. They live moment to moment, and being open and present to her gave me the opportunity to practice the same. More importantly, I realized that I put my life on hold by thinking I should be involved in something other than what's happening!

Through this exercise, I realized how much of life I say *no* to. My husband suggested we go on a cruise to Mexico. My first reaction was, "*No*—I might get seasick, we would be gone too long, I don't have the right clothes and I've already been to Mexico." *Who is this?* My experiment gave me pause to look at all the excuses I created, and I wondered just how much of my life had been compro-mised by my internal stop sign. If you can believe it, it was hard to say *yes* to his wonderful offer, but I finally agreed to go because my agreement with myself was to say *yes*.

The cruise was great fun. I did not get seasick, it seemed like it ended too soon, I bought the clothes I

I imagine that yes is the only living thing.
E.E. CUMMINGS

To say yes, you have to sweat and roll up your sleeves, and plunge both hands into life up to the elbows. It is easy to say no, even if saying no means death.
JEAN ANQUILH

needed and I saw parts of Mexico I'd never seen before. In keeping with the spirit of *yes* I went parasailing, wave riding, snorkeling, and hiking, and I danced until my feet hurt. It sure feels good to say *yes* to life!

Even though I know this, the voices of conditioning still taunt me with a myriad of reasons to say *no,* to stay put, to not take risks, not expand my life, not try something new. I can listen to the voices that tell me "slow down," "be careful," "I can't" or "I'll be hurt"—or I can choose to trust and go with the flow.

We are each moving at the speed of life, which is always the speed that is perfect for us. Notice what life offers you and remind yourself to say *yes*. You may be surprised and delighted with what happens next.

Ready to move out of your comfort zone?

~ Make a commitment to say *yes* to whatever comes your way for the next week. Notice your resistance, your need to stay in control, your unwillingness to trust life.

~ Notice what happens when you say *yes*.

~ How do you feel when you say *no*?

~ What are your inner voices saying? Is this true? How do they know?

~ At the end of your experiment, notice how saying *yes* has impacted you.

~ Now try it for another week, and another, and another.

Follow Your Bliss

AVE YOU LOST THE ability to surprise yourself? Has your life become predictable? *Or* is your pilot light burning brightly, ready to ignite with the next great adventure?

Making the next 50 your Best 50 is about accepting responsibility for how you show up for the rest of your life. Over our lifetimes, many women put their personal dreams and desires on hold in order to raise a family, help their sick or disabled parents, or for any number of valid reasons. We think, "Maybe *someday* when the kids are grown, when I'm financially secure, when I feel better—*then* I'll go to Africa; I'll volunteer; I'll rent a cabin in the mountains and paint, or write, or sculpt. I'll join the Peace Corp, start my own business, teach, or open a yoga center."

Well, here you are! *Someday* is now. At this stage of life, your kids are grown, or close to it. You've established your career; maybe you're even getting ready to retire or slow down. You know your own mind; you've earned your independence; and you're clear that having more stuff is

Dreams are renewable. No matter what our age or condition, there are still untapped possibilities within us and a new beauty waiting to be born.

REV. DR. DALE TURNER

Take charge of your future. If your ship does not come in, get off the beach and swim out to it.

UNKNOWN

What would you attempt to do if you knew you could not fail?

DR. ROBERT H. SCHULLER

not the road to happiness. You've looked your mortality in the face—and you could see it! *Now* is all we have. If the desire to rekindle your dream is starting a fire in your belly, this is the time to honor it.

Many of us don't tend to appreciate our own gifts and talents because they come so naturally to us. We don't have to work hard at them, and if it isn't difficult, it has no value, right? *There's* a limiting belief! Something that comes easy is the very definition of talent! Now is the time to take it to the next level. That's not to say you must only do what you're good at. Try new things, experiment—and choose the activities that bring you joy and happiness.

If you find yourself an empty-nester, you can now shift out of your caretaking roles and finally turn your attention to taking care of your*self*. Some women struggle with this transition, feeling stuck in the nurturing roles they know so well. All too often, a woman's sense of identity and value is wrapped up in how we care for others. Be gentle but firm with yourself and explore new ways to honor your emerging self.

In her book *The Wisdom of Menopause*, Dr. Christiane Northrup writes,

> As a woman enters menopause, she steps out of the primarily childbearing, caretaking role that was hormonally scripted for her. This is not to say that the postmenopausal woman is no longer an effective nurturer. Rather, she becomes freer to "color outside the lines…. Many of the issues that had become blurry to her when the hormones of puberty kicked in may suddenly resurface with vivid clarity as those hormones recede. This is why so many midlife women recall, and decide to confront, past abuses. The concern with social injustices, the political interests, and the personal passions that were sublimated in the

childbearing years now surface in sharp focus, ready to be examined and acted upon. Some women funnel this heightened energy into new businesses and new careers. Some discover and cultivate artistic talents they never knew they had. Some women note a surge in their sexual desire, to heights never before experienced in their lives. Some report changes in sexual preference.[66]

Clearly, midlife is a time of great opportunity! Allow yourself to dream big… and to follow those dreams. Beware of those inner voices that call you selfish, uncaring, and inconsiderate for thinking outside the box. Do not believe them. Heck, smash that box! It's just those nasty voices within trying (yet again) to convince you that there is something wrong with you. This time in your life was *meant* to shift your attention from nurturing your own family to broader concerns for the family of humankind.

Find a cause or concern that you are passionate about, and if you choose, become a volunteer. You've accrued a lot of skills along the way that can be put to good use. Give your time, attention, money or talents to a cause or organization that needs just what you have to offer. Don't do it because you have to or you should—do it because to do otherwise would feel like you were being untrue to what makes you—*you!* Giving takes you where striving "to get" never will.[67]

Following your dream is tantamount to nourishing your soul, the very essence of who you are. When a person begins to dream again, those dreams often come with a powerful itch to shake things up. It's not uncommon for women at this stage to consider leaving their life partner, career or hometown. This is especially common once those chickens have flown the coop. While

The greatest tragedy in life is not death; the greatest tragedy takes place when our talents and capabilities are underutilized and allowed to rust while we are still living.

AMMA

If you think you are too small to be effective, you have never been in a dark room with a mosquito.

UNKNOWN

Most people live and die with their music still unplayed. They never dare to try.
MARY KAY ASH

Your talent is God's gift to you. What you do with it is your gift back to God.
LEO BUSCAGLIA

for some this degree of change may be long overdue, it's certainly not necessary in order to live your dreams. There is another option: perhaps you just need a sabbatical!

A sabbatical is a defined period of time away from the demands of everyday life in a desired location in order to fulfill a longing of yours. It doesn't have to be a midlife crisis (is growing older really a crisis?) or a trial separation; it's simply time to go within and take care of *you*.

This is not selfish, so don't allow your inner voices (or your partner or family) to heap piles of guilt, shame or torment upon you. After so many years of self*less* giving, you can now be of service to others by honoring the whisperings of your own soul. Fulfilling your dream adds to the collective good of all of us. Your contribution might make a huge difference in the lives of others, help them awaken, and give them the courage to act and fulfill their own dreams. Sadly, by not living your dream, it will simply wilt on the vine—or grow in someone else's garden.

Academics and artists are known to take time away from everyday life to write, paint, sit still, ponder, and *be* without having to accommodate someone else. Even the Bible suggests we hold the seventh day for rest and allow the fields to lie fallow every seventh year. Surely the Divine would encourage you to take time to rest and rejuvenate.

Do you have a "Things to Do before I Die" list? If not, perhaps it's time to put one together and take action. Do something you've always dreamed about: take a solo trip to a foreign country; spend time in a warmer climate; teach a subject you're passionate about; volunteer in a third-world country; take an extended spiritual retreat; drive across America; take time to learn a new language, bird watch, write, draw, sing, dance, paint, sculpt or whatever your big heart desires! Remember, our dreams and creative juices don't dry up with age.

I had harbored a secret yearning for years, thinking I would never be able to fulfill it because I was married and had "responsibilities." I forgot that my primary responsibility in life is to always honor my own well-being! When my "hormonal veil" finally lifted, it became clear that I could no longer sacrifice myself to someone else's version of who I should be.

Time to Retreat

Throughout my life, I often fantasized about what it would be like to live as a monk in a monastery. (Tells you a lot about my fantasy life, doesn't it?) I love solitude, and an extended retreat was one of the things on my "To Do Someday" list.

At age 56, I wondered what I was waiting for. Would there ever be a perfect time to go? Why keep fantasizing? Why not just do it? I pondered. I talked with others about it. I was terrified, afraid that I might be different when I returned home. Maybe I wouldn't want to come back. Maybe my husband wouldn't want me back. Was I being selfish? Was I crazy?

To counter my state of confusion and indecision, I opened myself for guidance and sank into that centered, still place inside me. I took a walk along the ocean and, while strolling barefoot across the beach, came upon a flock of seagulls. Typically, when someone approaches, the birds flap their wings and noisily scatter to the skies. I braced myself for this chaos—but it was not to be. Maintaining my stride, I walked directly into the midst of the flock. To my surprise, *not one flew away*. Not only did they stay earthbound—they were actually quietly

When you are convinced that all the exits are blocked, either you take to believing in miracles or you stand still like the hummingbird. The miracle is that the honey is always there, right under your nose, only you were too busy searching elsewhere to realize it. The worst is not death but being blind, blind to the fact that everything about life is in the nature of the miraculous.

HENRY MILLER

waddling along beside me! I was so touched that I stopped in wonder—and cried… very hard.

I took it as a sign that I was walking the right path for me, and that I wasn't walking it alone. I learned it wasn't necessary to change my stride for anyone or anything, and that the things I fear usually don't come to pass. I understood that while life doesn't always meet my expectations, it often exceeds them when I get out of my own way. Yes, it was clearly time to honor my deepest desire for an extended spiritual retreat. I consider it a gift I gave myself.

After all the internal wrestling I had done with this desire, the decision came in such a sweet moment of grace. This experience was a profound reminder that when you release the question from your mind and open your heart to the answer, you will be shown the way.

My conditioned mind fought me tooth and nail, but I went ahead and made arrangements to live in silence at a monastery for three months. (It just seemed like the right place and the right amount of time for me.)

At the monastery, everything was structured to support me in living mindfully. I lived by a set schedule of meals and daily work assignments, and I meditated regularly and often. We cultivated, prepared, and dined on homegrown, organic, vegetarian food. I washed cartloads of dishes, all the while listening to my ego tell me I could have done this at home! I stuck with it. I was gradually beginning to understand that joy is in the *mindful doing*, not in the *done*.

I was supported with love and compassion as I constantly wrestled with my ego's need to be in control. Through this process, I finally understood my nagging fear of dying. It wasn't the authentic me who feared dying; it was my conditioned ego that feared the end of *its* reign was near. The more I lived in the moment, the more I paid attention, the less power it had over me. Who would have thought that such a structured setting could be so liberating?

Spending time at the monastery was both the hardest and the best thing I have ever done. It gave me a chance to be with myself, with no outside demands on my time or energy, in a structured and guided environment. It was an opportunity to explore the unconscious meanderings of my mind and get reacquainted with my sacred center.

It was also an opportunity to witness the choices I made on a daily basis and fully comprehend the consequences of those choices. All my life I have espoused a belief in the Divine, and it was difficult to acknowledge how little I actually trusted that belief. It was painful to see how much of my everyday life was spent in service to my conditioning, and how little trust I really had in God, in people, in life itself.

Oddly enough, it was a challenge to be in the presence of all that love, acceptance and compassion. My ego struggled for control in an environment where that was not supported. It told me I shouldn't be there, didn't deserve to be there, wasn't good enough. It was difficult to turn that toxic tide, difficult to find that place of quiet worthiness. But in the presence of all that love, acceptance and compassion, there were moments of clarity.

The true gifts came when I *knew* that regardless of what my conditioning would say, I am good, kind, lovable, compassionate, creative, smart, funny, talented and blessed. If you sit still long enough to listen, you too can hear the real truth about yourself (and it's *not* the one programmed into you and maintained by the voices of your conditioning). It was only when I resisted these truths that I became unhappy, fatigued and resentful. In those moments of graceful acceptance, I felt non-separate, at one with all that is. I knew that *this* is the space where life is truly lived.

Feel yourself being quietly drawn by the deeper pull of what you truly love.
RUMI

One sunny afternoon after lunch, while walking down a wooded lane on the way to my hermitage, I suddenly felt—*beautiful*! It just bubbled up from within, and it certainly had nothing to do with how I looked. I wore loose, comfortable clothing, no makeup, and hadn't seen a hairdryer in weeks. No amount of hair color or beauty products or primping had ever made me feel this way, not even close. This feeling emanated from deep inside. It was a direct experience of being full of beauty and well-being, of my spirit being connected with all of life. I was not separate.

I had felt attractive before, but it had always been tied to the way I looked. Other people had told me I was beautiful, but I never quite believed them because I didn't really *feel* beautiful. Those remembrances fell away in the face of this new understanding.

This understanding was like a seed that was planted at birth and finally given enough food and water to bloom. Though I had never felt this kind of beautiful before, it didn't feel foreign; it felt right, natural, *authentic*.

I believe every one of us was born with this seed. We simply have to sit still, pay attention and embrace the truth of it. Here I was, a silver-haired, 50-something woman in comfy couture experiencing the feeling of real beauty for the first time. My heart was full of gratitude as I turned my face to the sun and smiled widely, with tears trickling down my cheeks. I finally understood that *this* is the experience so many women are chasing at the cosmetic counters. (Ladies, it's not there.) That sense of true beauty remains deep within me and I am able to access it whenever I choose. It's there in you too.

So, follow your heart, listen to your internal yearnings. Give a voice to your secret longings and dreams. They can open you to realizations and possibilities that currently exist just beyond your awareness. While at the monastery,

I learned to stop trying to *make* things happen, to sit still, pay attention and allow my next step to reveal itself. (Turns out, it was writing this book!)

When you take steps to acknowledge what is true for you, you reconnect with your authentic self. When you do what you love, you are engaged, impassioned and present! While, given a lifetime of programming, it may not be easy to be the authentic you, it is as simple and necessary as breathing. Unzip the shroud of the self you've always tried to be and step forth into the freedom of who you truly are.

Never believe it's too late or you're too old. Laura Ingalls Wilder didn't begin to write her *Little House* books until she was in her 50s; Martha Graham danced until she was 76, and Georgia O'Keeffe kept painting well into her 90s. You go, girls! Er… ladies.

How can you give birth to your dream?

~ Close your eyes and go within. Take several slow, deep breaths. Imagine a yellow light entering your body through the crown of your head and swirling slowly down to your toes, filling you with a golden glow. Continue to take relaxing, deep breaths.

~ Draw this yellow light to the area just behind your navel and allow it to settle there, relaxing and warming you. In this still, receptive place, ask yourself, "If I could go anywhere and do anything, what would that look like? And for how long?" Stay with your dream as long as you can, noticing all the details—sights, sounds, activities, smells and tastes. Allow anything and everything to surface.

~ Notice if your inner voices are giving you flack and telling you that you can't be, have or do what you desire. These voices most likely reflect

Stop leaving and you will arrive. Stop searching and you will see. Stop running away and you will be found.
LAO TZU

Don't ask yourself what the world needs. Ask yourself what makes you come alive and then go do that. Because what the world needs are people who have come alive.
DR. HOWARD THURMAN

emotions you are unwilling to feel or limiting beliefs you hold. What are they telling you? Do you choose to believe them?

~ If emotions well up, simply allow them to surface. Feel them, express them if you need to, and put them to rest.

~ After you have a clear picture of what your dream looks like, write it down in detail. What would you be doing? Where? For how long?

~ Sit with your dream and savor it. Imagine yourself being there. See yourself fully engaged and notice how you feel.

~ Next, take practical steps to make it happen.

How? It's not important to know all the logistics just yet, but you do need to cultivate support. Birthing a dream needs a midwife. Talk with your partner or a close friend and ask for their support. From a centered place, share how important your dream is to you. If they feel threatened, assure them it is not about abandoning them; it is about honoring you. Together, brainstorm ways to get the ball rolling and make it happen for you.

Truth or Consequences

Many women hesitate to take steps toward their dreams because they harbor fears about how their partner or family will react. I knew that an extended retreat was very important to me, for both my sanity and my spiritual well-being. I also feared that my husband might leave me because of it. (I was going for 3 months!) I had to ask myself some very tough questions. If he didn't want me to go, would I abandon the experience my soul was longing for? Could I do that without resentment and continue to be in a loving relationship with him? Did I want to spend

Leap, and the net will appear.

JULIE CAMERON

Opportunity stands beside you every moment, and one of its favorite disguises is that of obstacles.

UNKNOWN

the rest of my life with someone who didn't support me in being all that I am?

I finally concluded that at this stage of my life, I was better off in a healthy relationship with myself than an unsupportive one with someone else. I was no longer willing to be who someone else wanted or needed me to be. I was at peace with my decision and willing to accept the consequences. From this place, I approached him with my intention to go away on retreat. He encouraged me to follow my heart. I went. He stayed.

My husband is a wise man and used the opportunity to create his own personal at-home retreat. He learned he could cook (I use the word loosely), do laundry, run his own errands and still get his work done. He began a workout program, lost the extra weight he'd been carrying, built some strength and became more self-sufficient (hallelujah!) We both came out of the experience feeling satisfied that we had done the right thing. We also developed a deeper appreciation for one another's individuality.

When I stand before God at the end of my life, I would hope that I would not have a single bit of talent left, and could say, "I used everything you gave me."

ERMA BOMBECK

Discover your dreams and consequences. Ask yourself:
~ What are the benefits of following my dream?
~ What are the consequences?
~ What might be the downside if I *do not* follow my heart?
~ Am I willing to honor my innermost longings?
~ If not, why not?
~ If so, when?

It's interesting to note that just when women are wanting to explore new possibilities and stretch our wings to see what more life can offer, many men are growing weary of being out in the world and want nothing more than to come home to roost. This can be a difficult time for any marriage. The forces that brought you together earlier in life have evolved. Through the crucible of your marriage, you must begin to create something new.

Quite frankly, a lot of couples will not survive this midlife rite of passage without a commitment to clear and honest communication. Old roles and responsibilities are often renegotiated; expectations change; the balance of power can shift. Dynamics that were tolerated in the past now become intolerable. Perhaps you've noticed this happening to you? For example, I had to become quite vocal about not being interrupted by my husband while I am writing. It seemed there was an unspoken belief (held by *both* of us) that his work was more important than mine, and that is no longer acceptable to me. Owning my part and expressing my concern allowed us to come to a better understanding and respect one another's time.

The consequences of capitulation can be disastrous. Women whose dreams lie fallow and who feel diminished or devalued in their relationships must speak their truth. The fallout of not doing so may be years of unhappiness and ill health. Remember, the body will manifest in symptoms whatever you refuse to allow into consciousness.

Peace is not the absence of conflict; it's the absence of inner conflict.

UNKNOWN

Ask yourself: *What is the cost of being untrue to myself, living a lie, pretending to be someone I'm not, or pretending to want something I've grown beyond?*

Then listen for your answer.

Working 10 'til 2

Sixty-six percent of baby boomers intend to work for pay after retirement, some from necessity, some by choice.[68] If you are interested in a new career, there couldn't be a better time. That loud sucking sound you'll hear over the next 15 years will be the vacuum caused by almost 76 million baby boomers retiring. With only 44 million GenXers to take their place, we're facing some serious labor pains! Many industries will have to be flexible and creative in order to attract enough employees. The law of (labor) supply and demand will create very favorable conditions for boomers who want to work, but not too much.

Unfortunately, many organizations have yet to see the writing on the wall. Sooner than later, the realization that more workers are going out the door than coming in will hit them, and they will be offering boomers opportunities we only fantasized about when we were younger. Many of us will want part-time opportunities, flexible schedules, and liberal time off for travel and hanging out with the grandkids… and many of us are going to get it. So find a career you've always wanted to try, and go for it. They'd be a fool to turn you away.

If all the world's a stage…
Some are working backstage,
Some are playing in the orchestra,
Some are on-stage singing,
Some are in the audience applauding,
And some are there as critics.
Know who and where you are.
UNKNOWN

"Self-Improvement"—Who Needs It?

As we cross over into new possibilities, it's important to understand that we are not trying to improve ourselves, but rather express the authentic self that is already there— intact, whole, capable, intelligent and wise.

How much of our precious life energy is squandered because we *believe* the stories we tell ourselves about our supposed inadequacies? *You're not good enough. You're a failure. You never do it right.* We are repeatedly told by our inner voices that we are not meeting a certain standard; that we'd better try harder. So, we do. We try and try to do all the things that society says will make us better, accept- able, and worthy, and yet our inner voices continue to tell us that we're still not good enough.

If you've found yourself trudging away on the treadmill of self-improvement, it might serve you to ask which "self" you are trying to improve. The ego self? The product of years of faulty conditioning?

The underlying assumption of self-improvement is that there is something *wrong* with us that needs fixing! Who said so? The conditioned ego. (Not a reputable source.) Our ego identities would have us believe there is *always something wrong* (with us, others, the world) and that there is *never enough* (love, money, time, resources).

Well, here's a radical idea. What if there is no self to improve? If you look at who you *really* are—the true, authentic you—you'll see that you're not defective or broken, and you never were. There are wounded aspects of you that need to be embraced and accepted, and there's the chatter of your conditioning.

That's it.

Once you silence all the inner voices that loudly proclaim your inadequacy, who is left?

In the stillness, you will know.

We do not have to improve ourselves; we just have to let go of what blocks our heart.

JACK KORNFIELD

CHAPTER 16

A Code You Can Live By

S OME PEOPLE KNOW EXACTLY what they want. Following their bliss is relatively easy because they have a well-developed sense of purpose and direction. It's like they somehow got a sneak peak at the roadmap of their journey—something the rest of us missed out on! Lacking this innate direction, most of us make our way forward in life relying on two basic, but often unconscious, tools of navigation: our values and our intentions.

We all live our lives rooted in a sense of personal values. It's just that most of the time, they haven't been consciously chosen and are simply a result of our conditioning. Many of us put our lives on cruise control until we come to a crossroads that requires us to wake up, choose a direction and grab hold of the steering wheel.

Approaching midlife could well be one of those crossroads. As we stand ready to open the door to the rest of our life, we have a choice. We can move forward on autopilot, dutifully carrying the past into the future, or

Nobody grows old merely by living a number of years. We grow old by deserting our ideals. Years may wrinkle the skin, but to give up enthusiasm wrinkles the soul.
SAMUEL ULLMAN

we can assess our life to be sure every step aligns with the things we value and intend for our life *now*.

Values are the aspects of life that you hold in high esteem; they are overarching principles that represent or reflect the things that are desirable, useful and important to us, or that bring meaning into our lives. Examples include:

Kindness	Reflection	Fitness
Fun	Authenticity	Non-violence
Generosity	Solitude	Silence
Respect	Compassion	Adventure
Connection	Mindfulness	Honesty
Purposeful work	Service	Freedom
Introspection	Simplicity	Sustainability

Everyone follows their own code of values; they are intensely personal and they influence our decisions and determine our actions.

For most of us, our values evolve over time. What you value at age 25 are not necessarily the same things you hold dear at 50. Perhaps white-knuckle adventure is not as important to you as it once was, yet you still go on advanced rafting trips instead of kayaking in the streams. You've come to appreciate solitude and stillness, but your life hasn't quite caught up yet. Or maybe you deeply value creativity and independence, but you're still maintaining someone else's books instead of building the business of your dreams. Getting in touch with your values can help you realign your life in ways that are both inspiring and deeply rewarding. When you are clear about the code you live by, every decision comes easier.

In order to create a fresh start, it's essential to uncover what's important to you *now*.

~ Brainstorm a list of ten or more values you wish to live by. Remember, your values may evolve over time, so be sure your list reflects where you are at *this* stage of life.

~ Distill your list down to the five core values that you consciously choose to guide you going forward.

~ Where might your life be reflecting old values that no longer nourish you?

~ What aspects of your life are in alignment with your current values, and where are you getting stuck?

_____ _____

_____ _____

_____ _____

_____ _____

_____ _____

As I worked on my own list of values, it occurred to me that I never once thought to write down *attractiveness, pleasing others*, or *looking younger*. Interesting.

Beware of the "But" Factor

What stops people from living in alignment with their deepest values?

It goes something like this:

"Yes, I value connection, *but* I just can't let go of what he did to me." (And you continue to feel resentful and alone.)

> Achieving genuine happiness may require bringing about a transformation in your outlook, your way of thinking, and this is not a simple matter.
> **TENZIN GYATSO, THE 14th DALAI LAMA**

"Sure I value purposeful work, *but* it's too late for me to change jobs at this stage of life." (And you suffer through long days of meaningless work.)

"I value silence and introspection, *but* my life is too busy to sit still." (And you live in a frazzled, anxious, stressed-out state.)

Everything that follows a "but" is a limiting belief, usually the result of an unmet or threatened need. The unmet need (*shelter, safety, social needs or esteem*) typically activates a *belief* (*it's too late for me*) that causes us to unconsciously override the value, keeping us stuck in old patterns that no longer serve us.

Explore the beliefs that keep you from living your five core values.

Example: *I value (fitness) but (I can't exercise because it hurts my back).*

- I value _____
   but _____

   _____

   _____

- I value _____
   but _____

   _____

   _____

- I value _____
   but _____

   _____

   _____

Delve into the truth of your "but" statements. *Is it really too late? Can you really not forgive? Is aerobic dance truly your only option to stay fit?* Change your "I can't" to

"I won't" to see if you can find the willingness to move beyond the limitation.

Be Intentional

We each have the choice to create the life we want through intention, rather than through attachment. Coming from intention, we do things because we choose to do them. Coming from a place of attachment, we do things because we are driven to do them.

Intentions set the broad context for your life. They are what you expect your life to reflect, even if you don't know how it will come to be. You simply need to give rise to your vision and give it permission to flourish. Being clear on the qualities you want your life to reflect allows things to unfold in ways you never would expect. Possibilities will arise, and the power of grace is at your service.

Some people confuse goals with intentions, thinking they are the same thing. Far from it! Goals are useful, but they are future oriented and focused on what you are going to *do* to achieve a certain outcome.

Examples:
I lose 15 pounds by my next class reunion.
I walk for 30 minutes a day, 4 days a week.

Each of these statements focuses on a future, measurable outcome, and encourages you to organize your time and activities in order to achieve that outcome. The primary focus is still on the future: whether you will reach your goal or not, what you will do or how you will feel when it is accomplished. We either reach our goals and wonder, "*Now what?*" or don't reach them and wonder, "*Now what?*" It seems we get to the same place either way!

Setting an intention is different than setting a goal because it allows you to determine the context in which you live your life. It speaks to the *now*, how you choose to *be* in the present moment.

When values and intentions intersect, people are unstoppable. Every creative force in the universe steps up to help. It's an opportunity to see the law of attraction at work. However, when we set an intention that conflicts with a core value, we feel out of integrity and unknowingly sabotage ourselves. This is why it's absolutely essential to be in touch with your own values and understand your "but" factor before setting a clear intention.

Kindness is more important than wisdom, and the recognition of this is the beginning of wisdom.

THEODORE RUBIN

What are your intentions for the rest of your life?

~ Write three intentions for your life, using all or some of the five values you selected as most important to you now.

Example: If your values were *creativity, mindfulness, kindness, accountability* and *compassion,* your intentions might read:

My intention is to be kind to myself and others, regardless of circumstances.

I intend to live mindfully and own my experience.

I creatively express my innermost self (through dance, music, painting, etc.).

_____

_____

_____

_____

_____

_____

~ *Hint:* If you are having a difficult time coming up with your values, write down your intentions and your values will become evident!

How can you use your intentions to help you live more fully in the present?

When we encounter a difficult or confusing situation, or are bowled under by the negative messages from within, these intentions can serve as beacons to guide our choices. We then regain our ability to make decisions that are in sync with our highest good.

If you accept the premise that our thoughts are like magnets, drawing to us whatever we focus on, then *intentions* are akin to a gentle tap on the shoulder, a reminder to awaken and notice what you're thinking, what you're doing, and how you are being in the moment. That gentle tap on the shoulder brings you back to *now* rather than *now what*?

When I became clear on what I valued and set my intention to experience more of it, life just naturally started to move in that direction. It's like throwing out a lifeline and hooking it on to your vision. A path opens up before you, and previously unseen forces pull you in a direction you are fully prepared to go.

✾

The good life, as I conceive it, is a happy life.
I do not mean that if you are good you will be happy—
I mean that if you are happy you will be good.

BERTRAND RUSSELL

CHAPTER 17

The Happiness Quotient

I F YOU ASK PEOPLE what they truly want out of life, most answers boil down to one thing: "I just want to be happy." The good news is that the older we become, the easier it is to achieve that goal. As we age we become more conscious of the fact that time is running out, and we are reluctant to waste precious time and energy on things that are really not all that important.

In the January 2005 issue of *Psychology Today*, Carlin Flora suggests that living in the present may be the key to happiness. Her article cites research by Dr. Richard Davidson that indicates meditation may actually change how the brain works. In a study of people who had completed an eight-week meditation training, he found a significantly greater amount of activity in their prefrontal cortex, the part of the brain associated with positive feelings and pursuit of goals.

Flora also suggests that we all have a happiness "set point" determined by our innate temperament and our experiences early in life. Each of us has had moments of absolute delight after reaching a goal or seeing a long-

*Happiness—
to be dissolved into
something complete
and great.*
WILLA CATHER

anticipated desire come to fruition, but after it's been realized, we typically settle back into the same level of happiness that we've always had.

This highlights a major defect in our thinking: the "if only" defect." "*If only* I had (fill in the blank), *then* I'd be truly happy. *If only* so and so would just (fill in the blank), *then* I'd be happy. *If only* I had more (fill in the blank), *then* I wouldn't have to worry."

This is not new information. It's just that so many of us become so enmeshed in this grand illusion to some degree that it bears repeating. It's especially relevant to revisit this process when we are wrestling with the fears of growing older. By not recognizing the pattern, we are doomed to repeat it—and we don't have time for this nonsense!

The basic root of happiness lies in our minds; outer circumstances are nothing more than adverse or favorable.

MATHIEU RICARD

Make a list of your "if only" thoughts.

Here are a few examples to get you started.

If only…	**Then I'd be…**
I had large breasts	*desirable*
I was married	*secure*
I was thin	*attractive*
I wasn't married	*free to explore my creativity*
I was younger	*happier*
_____	_____
_____	_____
_____	_____
_____	_____

"If only—then I" is a recipe for unhappiness and suffering. Relying on our external circumstances for our internal sense of happiness will not work. What we are saying is that our life has to fit our picture of what we *think* it ought to look like in order to be happy.

Fortunately, assuming we have a balanced ratio of the necessary brain chemicals, we can raise our happiness thermostat a few degrees by understanding that our sense of well-being is tied to our perception of time. When you are fully present for your life, your experiences fill up the moments, making them seem much richer and deeper. While you have the same amount of time as everyone else, it *feels* like you have more because you are really present for it. It's the difference between gulping down a chocolate bar and barely tasting it, or mindfully savoring the chocolate as it slowly melts across your tongue. Either way, you've eaten the same amount of chocolate.

Flora writes, "*...the finding suggests that if we train ourselves to become more mindful and slow down our sense of passing time, we can learn to monitor our moods and thoughts before they spiral downward. We can, in other words, make ourselves happier.*"[69]

By staying with whatever is happening in the moment, we become aware that we can choose to follow the familiar path of negativity or do otherwise, thus becoming happier.

You people in the West make it too difficult. If you want to be happy, stop doing the things that are bad for you and start doing the things that are good for you.
TENZIN GYATSO, THE 14th DALAI LAMA

Choosing a Perspective

Researchers who have studied centenarians notice that one trait they all seem to have in common is an ability to see the glass as half-full. Those of us who accept responsibility for our *experience* of life and adopt positive attitudes really do live longer and have healthier lives![70]

Sometimes, looking at the dark side of humanity, it's not easy to keep a positive outlook. Terrorism, cruelty, indifference to our planet's health, and politicians focused on their own ambition can make us want to turn away in disgust. How do we make sense of all this negativity

Take one step at a time toward sanity and backtrack to where the gender balance went awry and begin to ask the question: "Where is the feminine perspective in the major decision-making processes for global health and sustainability, and why is she so silent?"

JANE EVERSHED

People never think of happiness as a way of being because they are thinking of pleasure, which depends on circumstances.

MATTIEU RICARD

and not allow it to poison our spirit? It's all in your perspective.

Yes, there are a lot of terrible things in the world. So much of our media coverage is focused on "what's wrong" that it can literally wipe the smile right off your face. Train your mind not to dwell there.

I'm not suggesting you turn your back on the ills of the world or pretend there aren't some serious problems to be solved. Be informed, be proactive, but remember that a mind can only take so much disturbing news before it goes into overload. Sometimes we just have to turn off the TV, ignore the daily paper, disconnect from the political blogs and choose to spend time on something positive. Constantly bathing your insides with fight-or-flight stress hormones will age you faster than Mother Nature ever intended.

Lift your own spirit. Focus on the good around and within you. Use meditation or centering prayer to help quiet the negative thoughts that create anxiety, fear and worry. Find a process that helps you deeply relax your mind and body. Nurturing a sense of peace within allows us to carry that attitude and mindset out into the world.

Once you are centered and in charge of your experience, take action. We can't fix everything, but we can remedy *something*. Find a cause or issue or project you feel passionate about and *do* something. Find a way to make a difference. Volunteer. Engage in random acts of kindness. Be generous.

Here's an intriguing *koan* (a paradox used to train the minds of Zen Buddhist monks) I chewed on for a long time before I understood it:

If you want to be happy—be happy!

What!?

Try something:

- ∼ Close your eyes for a moment and remember a time when you were happy.
- ∼ Smile, feel it, take a deep breath and know… that experience of happiness is *always* within you! In essence, you already know what it feels like to be happy. The feeling is accessible to you any time you choose. We just forget to choose!

By not being dependent on anything external to be happy—we can *be* happy! Happiness is an inside job and can be felt *regardless* of your circumstances. It's all about embracing the moment and being grateful for whatever is happening.

I can just imagine what the voices of conditioning are saying to you at this minute. Do you choose to believe them?

Happiness is not a place to *get to*, but a place to *live from*. It's a mindset, a feeling of being engaged with life, a willingness to side-step obstacles, find creative options, let go of the past and live in the present. It's a willingness to call on our own inner wisdom and remember there is only *here*, here.

Our lives are only a blip on the canvas of creation. Accepting the fleeting nature of our existence allows us to appreciate the impermanent, ever-changing, fluid journey we are on. *Now* is all we have.

Many of us believe there is a purpose to everything, although it is unlikely we will ever see it clearly. When it comes to determining whether something is good or bad, we simply don't have the perspective to know the whole truth. Perhaps nature's plan to dial down our physical prowess and beauty as we age is actually an invitation to explore our spiritual nature. Having lived these many years, we have inner reserves of wisdom and experience to

The person who seeks all their applause from outside has their happiness in another's keeping.
CLAUDIUS CLAUDIANUS

integrate and offer to the world. This is both the privilege and the responsibility of the Amazing Grays.

∞

I will not die an unlived life.
I will not live in fear of falling or catching fire.
I choose to inhabit my days, to allow my living to open me,
To make me less afraid,
More accessible, to loosen my heart
Until it becomes a wing, a torch, a promise.
I choose to risk my significance, to live so that which came to me
as seed
Goes to the next as blossom,
And that which came to me as blossom,
Goes on to fruit.

DAWNA MARKOVA

PART FOUR

SPIRITUAL
PERSPECTIVES

*Roots of a
Deeper Kind*

Human beings are a part of a whole called by us the "Universe," a part limited in time and space. We experience ourselves, our thoughts and feelings, as something separated from the rest—a kind of optical delusion of consciousness. This delusion is a kind a prison for us, restricting us to our personal desires and to affection for a few persons nearest us. Our task must be to free ourselves from this prison by widening our circles of compassion to embrace all living creatures and the whole of nature and its beauty.

ALBERT EINSTEIN

Roots of a Deeper Kind

MIDLIFE IS A TIME WHEN MANY of us grow tired of our preoccupation with youth and beauty and status. All around us are messages that encourage us to jump onto the treadmill of more, more, more. Ironically, doing so now seems to leave us with less, less, less—satisfaction, inner peace, and fulfillment. Turning inward and upward in our search for deeper meaning, we find ourselves wondering:

> *What is my purpose? How do I find it? How can I make the most of my time? Will there be enough? Will I be loved? Who am I now? Can I keep my physical body attractive and also discover the essence of who I am? Why are my looks so darned important? Is this all there is?*

The real secret of the Amazing Grays just might lie in their willingness to embrace a larger perspective, one that focuses not on one's changing physical form, but on deepening one's spiritual roots.

Paying attention to the moments of grace in life can empower us to live *authentically*. By finding ways to become more mindful (and understanding what that actually means), we can live more joyfully.

From sitting meditation to centering prayer, from yoga to rosary beads, there are many ways to practice clearing out the noise of everyday life and gracefully accepting "what is."

Being in the present moment doesn't necessarily mean you walk around with a blissful grin on your face at all times. (Although Thich Nhat Hanh, a Vietnamese Buddhist teacher, recommends you do just that. He suggests that as we smile, we send a message to our body to relax.) It means your response to the moment is authentic and accepting of what is actually happening *now*. More often than not, by surrendering and paying attention to your life as it unfolds, you will feel oh so satisfied.

Go ahead and smile—and notice how you feel.

CHAPTER 18

Turning Within

W HEN *NEWSWEEK* EXPLORED SPIRITU-
ALITY in America in the summer of
2005, a poll of 1,004 Americans found
that:

79% describe themselves as "spiritual"
64% say they are "religious"
66% engage in daily prayer
30% meditate daily

Of those who indicated that "spirituality was very
important in their daily lives," the percentage increased
with age, from 44 percent in the 18-39 age group, to over
two-thirds of those over age 60.[71]

The human quest for love, compassion, acceptance
and peace is universal—and deeply personal. The way
a person connects with a higher power is unique unto
them—whether it's religion, spirituality, or a quiet, private
sense of reverence. We may refer to this "power bigger
than ourselves" by different names, but the underlying
desire for connection with the Divine is a core thread in

*Who looks outside,
dreams; who looks
inside, awakes.*

CARL JUNG

many of our lives, and it seems to become more important as we grow older.

Many of us have spent a lifetime defining ourselves by what we look like and what we do. These aspects of ourselves gave us a sense of personal power and security. But now, our children are growing up and leaving the nest; retirement beckons; relationships evolve; our faces and bodies are changing; and we are forced to look elsewhere for the things that define us.

As we move into our silver years, many of us quietly reassess and redesign our quality of life by choosing to live more mindfully. As the demands of active careers and growing families lessen, we are moved to slow down, take a breath and consciously decide how we want to live our lives going forward. Regardless of one's particular faith, many of us are looking to deepen our connection with the Divine.

Spiritual Humans or Human Spirits?

At some level, we're all asking the same questions and reaching for the same connection. The human condition leaves us suspended between two perspectives, asking ourselves:

Am I a mere mortal looking for happiness and fulfillment through achievement of my goals and the accumulation of material goods while striving to be a person worthy of love, knowing that this is it?

OR,

Am I essentially a spiritual being here to experience life, love and humanity as it unfolds moment by moment and bring a gentler, wiser perspective to an earthly way of life?

I've always leaned toward the latter, yet I still wondered, "If I had the perfect body, partner, home, career and family, would my life be complete? Would I

The best things in life are nearest. Breath in your nostrils, light in your eyes, flowers at your feet, duties at your hand, the path just before you.

ROBERT LOUIS STEVENSON

be happy? If I am primarily a spiritual being, why are my looks so darn important to me? Can I work to keep my physical body attractive and also discover the essence of who I am? Am I simply a physical being put here to look good and collect toys? Could that really be all there is? What is the broader perspective? What gives my life purpose? Meaning?" These are valid and important questions, and the search for answers has certainly enriched my life. Asking questions shines a light on the unknown and allows me to explore possibilities.

Questions can be both stimulating and frightening at the same time, because they challenge the status quo. Once you open yourself up to new thoughts, it's difficult to go back to your old way of thinking. Knowledge changes us intrinsically, stretching our minds and beliefs to the point of no return. Trying to back up is like trying to put the toothpaste back in the tube—very messy, with limited success. But then again, why would you want to?

Exploring different perspectives and ideas allows us to choose which ones we want to identify with, which ones we want to experience. So, let's take a moment to examine this age-old debate: are you essentially a human or a spirit? Or both? Perhaps it all boils down to what you focus on.

The Human Perspective

The human perspective is predominately one of mind, body and emotion. From this point of view, we are defined by what we think, how we look and how we feel.

While we each share a physical blueprint with all other humans, our tendency is to see ourselves as separate and distinct. Seeing ourselves as separate from others, we compare ourselves to them. We spend a lot of time thinking about our place in society, and we work hard to maintain an image of power and capability, because down deep, we often feel like we're never quite "there." We turn to other humans for direction, always on the lookout for which standards of beauty and achievement our society values. If we meet the standard, we feel temporarily satisfied. If not, we feel less than. It's a process we come by honestly, as for much of our lives many of us are taught not to trust ourselves. Instead, we learn to turn to external sources of validation.

If we define our worth in terms of our looks, reproductive capabilities and sexual desirability, we often panic when those traits begin to change. We spend huge amounts of time, energy, and money trying to fix or hide our perceived flaws, always trying to be the *right* person, be seen with the *right* people, have the *right* stuff and, of course, do things *right*. Does any of this sound familiar? It takes a lot of effort to be human, doesn't it?

When I forget my eternal spiritual nature and define myself by my human attributes, fear takes over and the changes in my aging human body loom large and scary. I feel compelled to hang onto the past. (This is where the kicking and screaming part comes in.) I worry inordinately about the changes in my appearance, as if that's all I have to define *me*. The fear of growing older starts with the belief that getting old will be the end of *me* as I've always known myself: my power, my influence, my value, and yes, my ego.

For women who haven't nurtured a spiritual core to draw upon, who either don't know or forget that we are *way* more than physical beings, these thoughts can be terrifying. It's no wonder so many of us fear getting older.

What can we gain by sailing to the moon if we are not able to cross the abyss that separates us from ourselves?
THOMAS MERTON

Life shrinks or expands according to one's courage.
ANAIS NIN

The Spiritual Perspective

There is no denying that we are human beings with physical bodies—but I suspect that's not the heart of *who we are*. The spirit inhabits the body, but it is not the body. I experience divinity through my physical form: my body is simply a temporary vehicle for the spirit to move in the world; it's like a suit of clothing. From a spiritual perspective, it doesn't matter what the package looks like—it's the *essence* of a person that's important.

Spirit is an invisible force made visible in all life.
MAYA ANGELOU

I see aging gracefully as a process of gradually shifting my attention from the package to the essence. By accepting that I am actually a spirit inhabiting a human body, I can embrace the changes in my physical form with more grace than I might otherwise exhibit. This perspective helps me see beyond my very human fears and into a deeper and more meaningful process. It helps me entertain the notion that my "sacred space" is not a church or corner of my house, but my entire life.

An enlightened master was once asked how he spent his time before he became enlightened. He replied, "I chopped wood. I carried water." He was then asked how he spent his time now that he was enlightened. His reply: "I chop wood. I carry water."[72] Living from a spiritual perspective, we continue to do the same things we've always done, but with a different mindset. It's not about *what* you do, but about *how you relate* to it.

My spiritual perspective allows me to better appreciate that everything is exactly as it should be, and to see this with increasing awareness, acceptance, compassion, and joy. There is a growing understanding that "my passing thoughts are not who I am," and that these same patterns of thought are what stand between me and the joyful existence that is my birthright.

Embracing this wisdom allows me to laugh at myself, open my heart, and not take the trappings of the physical world quite so seriously. After all, looks change, careers evolve, houses get sold, relationships end, and shoes wear out. There is nothing to preserve, and everything to experience.

We are like bottles of fine wine. If we keep the bottle safe and cool in the cellar, out of the heat and light, and we constantly admire the shape of the bottle and beauty of the label without ever tasting and appreciating the wine inside, aren't we missing the point of why the wine was made in the first place?

Embracing the spiritual being that I know myself to be is like taking a big swig of life. With this perspective, I can see more clearly and embrace the road ahead with compassion and understanding—and, I trust, grace.

There are no guarantees, and the only real security lives deep within. Eventually, the courageous choose to dive into those depths to discover what is there.

The Bridge across Perspectives: Moments of Grace

As we move through life, many of us experience moments of extraordinary clarity. Subtle messages, whisperings, and intuitive leaps seem to come out of the blue to point us in a particular direction. Sometimes they're sparked by a person, event or conversation, and sometimes it's just a gentle stirring within. If we're willing to pay attention and listen, they offer the opportunity to see the world differently.

Our lives are graced with an intelligence that, when heeded, allows us to take ownership and consciously make choices that support us in living more fully—as who we really are. I have come to appreciate grace as *an unexpected and unsolicited gift of insight from a higher source that transforms us, allowing us to perceive things with fresh eyes.* If we surrender to these moments of grace, they take us softly by the shoulders and turn us to reveal options and perspectives that we couldn't see before.

As you know, it was a moment of grace that pulled my attention inward and allowed my fears around aging to surface. As I sat in the hair salon with a head full of toxic goop and foil antennae, something inside of me shifted in such a way that I could no longer deny the truth of what I was doing. I was slowly poisoning myself; resisting the natural progression of life; harboring fears about who I really was; and questioning my worth as an infertile woman.

In that flash of extraordinary clarity, I saw it all. And then the moment passed. In the seconds that followed, I had a choice: I could ignore what I had just seen, resist this transformative gift of insight, and discount it as a "weird experience," or I could embrace it as a gift from a higher source. That was the pivotal moment.

Shifting Realities

An earlier—and possibly even more transformative— moment of grace came during my early twenties as a college student in Chicago. It was 1969. Like most of my peers, I wore bell-bottom jeans with fringe along the hem and a delicately embroidered gossamer peasant blouse. An authentic Navy-issue pea coat was slung over one arm. My long brown hair was parted down the middle and fell nearly to my waist, and the now familiar peace sign adorned my ears. (I'll bet some of you remember that look well!)

It was a crisp October morning, sometime between English Lit and World History, and I was riding the

Grace fills empty spaces, but it can only enter where there is a void to receive it, and it is grace itself which makes the void.
SIMONE WEIL

elevator. When the doors opened on the fifth floor, in walked a disheveled, plain-looking girl, also in her early twenties. She wore a crushed, dirty coat and baggy pants, and her hair hung in clumps around her greasy forehead. She juggled an armful of books with papers sticking out in all directions, and her fingernails were grimy. She *reeked* of Ambush cologne. The doors closed and it was just the two of us.

I stood toward the back of the elevator, and with a clear view of her, I began to mentally judge and berate her without mercy. (Hey, I was 21). Her smell disgusted me, she wasn't the least bit fashionable, and she hadn't even combed her hair! She obviously didn't care about her hygiene or her appearance, or so I told myself. (At least I was a *clean* hippie.) I went on and on with the disparaging internal monologue, feeling quite smug and superior.

Suddenly, time seemed to stand still. I felt a subtle pressure on my ears and all external sound ceased, except for a faint buzzing. I felt like I was suspended in liquid light, but I was part of the light—*and so was she*! From nowhere in particular, a quiet voice whispered, "You are the same."

My "being-ness" and her "being-ness" became One and I was enveloped in a love so deep and pure I was dumbfounded. It was like standing naked in front of the world, with all my perceived shortcomings, imperfections and mistakes hanging out there for everyone to see, but instead of feeling chastised and judged, I experienced only unconditional love and acceptance—times ten! It was a feeling of being cherished, esteemed, valued and loved, and knowing I deserved that. Knowing I *am* that.

In that moment of clarity I "saw" that she and I were not separate. I was aware that as I judged her, I judged myself. The life force that animated her was the same life force that animated me and every other living thing. I was

When we try to pick out anything by itself, we find it hitched to everything else in the universe.

JOHN MUIR

filled with a love that seemed not of this world. Neither of us moved or did anything out of the ordinary; we didn't even make eye contact. Then, the elevator door opened and she walked out.

I remained in a state of awe and reverence for the rest of the day. History class was history. I left the building and walked along the Lake Michigan shoreline, marveling at the vibrant fall colors.

Everything seemed to shimmer with a golden glow and I felt a lightness of being, a kindness of heart, a true sense of not being separate from life itself. The people I encountered all seemed so dear. I was reminded of the continuity of life and the gossamer web of love that connects us all. I was transported into a profound state of awe at the beauty of the world around me. I now *knew* there was "something more" that connects us and that I was an integral part of life, not separate from it. I had a deep knowing that *Everything Is All Right.*

As I matured, I often forgot that "everything is all right," easily falling under the spell of my conditioning, and spending too much of my time and energy trying to be "enough" and prove that there was nothing wrong with me.

I do know, however, that if I had ignored or discounted this profound gift of grace, my life might have taken a much different turn. This experience and the insights I gained set my spiritual anchor and have served as my touchstone. Remembering that "everything is all right" allows me to embrace the aging process as the spiritual opportunity it truly can be.

Appreciating Your Moments of Grace

The inner voices of your conditioning are *not* the whisperings I am alluding to. While they are not the voice of the Divine, they would certainly like you to believe they are. It takes practice to know the difference.

Grace appears as a deep knowing, a sense of changing direction, an ethereal but tangible sense of purposeful intelligence. When I trusted myself enough to listen to these messages, they opened me up to unexpected opportunities and mysteries of life, and always guided me back to my authentic self.

Looking back on your life, can you recall some extraordinary moments when you were encouraged to change course? Sudden insights that led to unexpected choices and experiences? Synchronicities that were clearly not random? These moments of grace are profound, and whether dramatic or ordinary, they change us forever. When they come into your life, no matter how unusual, uncomfortable, or unsettling they seem, do not dismiss them. Grace is not an experience that one can prepare or ask for. Our best hope is to *pay attention* so that we might recognize these gifts when they are offered.

This is not always easy, especially in a Western culture of achievement, busyness and consumption. The fear of letting go of the familiar can freeze us in our tracks, causing us to ignore these callings. Once again we are faced with a moment of choice. Do we face the fear and trust the insight being offered, or do we settle into lives of quiet desperation, doing what we think we're *supposed* to do?

The good news is, opportunities abound. For many women, these whisperings seem to get louder during our menopausal years, which makes sense if you remember that this is a time in life when we're being physically

Sometimes your only available transportation is a leap of faith.

REV. MARGARET SHEPARD

rewired and new sensitivities are awakening. As we get older, it's more important than ever to tune in to this inner radar. It's essential to create space and time in our lives to listen, to feel, to explore, and to decide on a course of action. There isn't a lot of time left for do-overs.

Think back on your life and identify your moments of grace.

~ Did you heed the call? How did it transform you or open you up to new possibilities?

~ Were there times you ignored the insights offered?

~ Can you let go of any judgments, regrets, or sadness about these missed opportunities and know that you did the best you could at the time?

~ Are you sensing a call to action now? If you are ignoring it—what is your fear? What might happen if you follow it?

_____

_____

_____

_____

_____

_____

_____

Be careful not to compare your moments of grace with anyone else's. Each of us experiences life on our own terms and through our own filters. *Every* whisper of guidance is profound… simply yours for the taking (or not).

CHAPTER 19

The Workings of a Conditioned Ego

U NLESS YOU'RE A MYSTIC among us, you're probably not always attuned to the moments of grace that arise in your everyday existence. Most of us can't hear our whispers because of the ongoing static that runs between our ears—the endless chatter of our conditioning. While we've become familiar with our inner voices of discontent, let's take a deeper look at how they cause us to miss out on an authentic life. Understanding this process may just be the awareness we need to create the fresh start we've all been yearning for—giving us the wisdom to live moment to moment.

When I look back, there are huge chunks of my life that I simply can't recall. I've been given the glorious gift of life, and I don't remember a lot of it! That's sad. I can now see that I have spent much of my life in the trance-like, sleepwalking state that so many of us call "reality."

American Zen teacher Cheri Huber writes, "Life is glorious. Almost no one experiences life. We experience conditioned mind and think that's life."[73] The first time I read this, I was stunned. Then I felt a deep sadness as the truth of it sunk in. "Authentic life" lay hidden under a veil of false beliefs and assumptions created by our conditioned ego and sold to us as a bill of goods called "reality."

It seems many of us have fallen asleep to our true nature. You know what I'm talking about; you don't realize you've been in a trance until you snap out of it. It's like taking a walk and spending the majority of your time having a conversation in your head about something that happened in the past or has yet to happen in the future. Upon your return, you can't tell anyone what you saw, where you walked or even what the weather was like! The voices in your head distracted you from the present with loud stories about what might go wrong, what you need to do to stay safe, how you need to behave to be loved and accepted, what someone else should have said or done, and so on. Sadly, this adds up to weeks, and months, and years of your life… gone, in a cloud of mental chatter. This is a mindless existence rather than a mindful life.

Moving into your second (third?) act, don't you want to become aware of the players who've been running the show? Only by understanding that they are simply actors in your movie can you disengage from them and reclaim the authentic life that is your birthright.

This phenomenon—living through the mind, the conditioned ego—is addressed in almost every religion, spiritual tradition, and approach to psychology. They may use different words, but they all draw attention to the difference between the authentic self and the fabricated ego self. (In this discussion, the word "ego" does not reflect the Freudian definition, but rather the personality that develops from childhood conditioning.) What follows is a distillation of these various perspectives and a discussion about how we come to believe ourselves to be separate—from each other and from a Divine source. By understanding what has happened to our authentic self

The tragedy of life is not that it ends so soon, but that we wait so long to begin.

W.M. LEWIS

The great metaphors from all the spiritual traditions—grace, liberation, being born again, awakening from illusion—testify that it is possible to transcend the conditioning of my past and do a new thing.

SAM KEEN

we can begin the process of recovering it. Once you have tasted it, it becomes hard to settle for anything less.

The Die Is Cast

Many teachings suggest that when we're born, we don't experience ourselves as separate from the Divine, from life, from all that is. If you doubt this, spend time observing a very young child. You'll notice they live in the moment, experiencing everything as it happens. They are ego*less*. They have no agenda and love unconditionally. They cry when they're in pain, sleep when they're tired, eat when they're hungry and smile when they're happy. They fill their diapers with aromas that make others want to flee the premises, yet they experience no shame or embarrassment. They are curious about whatever is presented to them and go with the flow of life.

It's no wonder that many adults are so drawn to young children; they remind us of our natural state of being, our innocence, our oneness with all that is, our authenticity. It isn't until age three or four that our conditioning takes hold and slowly begins to mold us into fearful, anxious, and sometimes neurotic adults. *That* this happens I know; *why* it happens is for greater minds than mine.

So how do we go from authentic innocents to reactive, conditioned personalities? As we grow up and are socialized to "get along," we learn to negotiate for the love and attention we need to survive. As children, we are dependent on adults for the basic necessities of life; we know, at some level, that without adults we would die. To mitigate this concern, we quickly learn about cause and effect, developing patterns of thought and ways of seeing and interpreting the world based on our experience. *When I do this, I'm loved and seen as valuable. I can't do that or they won't want and/or love me. If I behave this way, I might be rejected. If I say that, they won't love me.*

Ultimately, as children, we struggle to be the right person in order to win our caregivers' approval and earn the love and attention we need to survive. When a need goes unmet, we become resourceful and try to figure out *who* or *how* to be in order to survive. To keep all the rules straight and be sure we're behaving like our caretakers want, the ego begins to form a personality of its own. Different aspects of that personality—sub-personalities—develop over time to meet our needs or deal with challenges as they arise. Have you ever heard someone claim that "a part of me wanted to do it, but another part was afraid"? These parts of us often battle for control.

If you listen carefully, most of us will find an internalized parent, commonly known as the "judge," who punishes us when we do, say or think something "bad" by telling us we are unworthy, stupid, careless or whatever adjective best crumbles our spirit. There is usually some version of a child who feels lost or abandoned. There is often a victim who feels powerless, and other personalities that arise as needed to cope with the challenges of life. These different parts of our psyches develop beliefs about how the world works and what we have to do to survive in it.

The voices in your head talk over every waking moment of your life, telling you what to do, what not to do, how to behave, what you should have said or done, how you messed up, that you can't do anything right, that there really is something wrong with you—and they're all *based on a child's belief of what she needed to do to survive.* (Yes, even the voice that just told you this isn't true.)

While it may seem otherwise, conditioning a child is not an intentionally cruel process, and in some ways it even seems necessary. After all, how else are we going to keep children from coloring on the walls or running into traffic?

Gradually we learn to behave in ways that will bring us love and spare us the pain of feeling separate and unworthy, *even if it means being untrue to ourselves.* The voices are so loud, so strong, that we learn to abandon our instincts and look to the world around us for what we should think, how we should behave, what we should expect. Eventually, we look to others for a sense of what is real and true, and we lose trust in ourselves. It's no wonder we're easy targets for the advertising industry! They exploit this basic aspect of the human condition to the advantage of their clients.

You Are Not Who You Think You Are

If power is intoxicating, the ego is often an obnoxious drunk.

The ego needs to be in control and thinks it knows what is best for you—and it can be very LOUD about getting its way. As this ego-based personality gets stronger, we begin to see ourselves as a separate identity. Eventually we forget we were ever *not* conditioned and come to think the egocentric conditioned self is who we are. We end up believing all our thoughts are true. After all, they've been there for as long as we can remember, right?

When we carry these unexamined patterns, fears and beliefs into our adult lives, and direct our energy and attention outward in an attempt to fit in, we lose touch with our internal compass. Our lives are gradually taken over by our conditioning and we lose the power to live our lives authentically… and don't even know it.

It's easy to get locked in to trying to be the *right* person who sees the world in the *right* way. We often defend our points of view by mocking, criticizing, poking fun at or shunning anyone who does not share or support them. We get locked in to the "us vs. them" mentality, the basis for so much suffering in this world.

As the years passed, I grew tired of this game. Through my awareness practice, I've become more secure in who I am, and I accept myself as a conditioned (yet perfectly imperfect) human being doing the best I can.

One day, while watching the *Wizard of Oz* for the umpteenth time with my granddaughters, it hit me—the conditioned ego is a lot like the Wizard of Oz! They both maintain power by staying hidden, scaring me with a lot of noise and threats, and convincing me to jump through hoops. They declare their power to be absolute, but when I pull aside the curtain of illusion, I can see that the wizard (conditioned ego) is really just a confused, powerless voice—nothing more than I make it.

As the Wizard himself proclaims in the movie, *"Pay no attention to the man behind the curtain!"* Good advice!

Your conditioned ego is *not* your friend! It has a chokehold on your authentic nature, and it will not let go until you expose it.

Here's the good news: We don't have to dig around in our past to understand where our conditioning came from. We don't even have to fix ourselves—we aren't broken! The first step to regaining our power is to pay attention to our inner voices, observe them and understand that they do not reflect who we *really* are.

Take a moment and illuminate your illusions.

~ Which characteristics or qualities do you believe you must have in order to be the "right person," worthy of other people's love and acceptance?

~ Which characteristics do you feel you must banish or hide? What "faults" are you ashamed of?

~ Who told you these qualities are good or bad? How do you know if that's true?

~ Who would you be if you stopped listening to these inner voices?

_____

_____

_____

_____

None of us really wants to live as the pawn of a conditioned ego on a power trip. What can we do? I found that when I asked simple questions, such as: *Who is this? How do you know this is true? Who told you this? Who says so?* I was able to disconnect from these negative inner messages and make room for a more centered, compassionate part of me to respond. While this may appear to be a simple solution, it is not an easy fix. Constant vigilance is required to strip the conditioned ego of its power to run (and ruin) your life. Then you can come from choice and respond rather than react to circumstances.

I have learned that the goal is not to get rid of the conditioned personality, but to quiet it down and make it transparent so you can see through it to your authentic nature.

Thankfully, we all have access to the truest part of ourselves, which remains intimately connected to our true nature. No matter what has happened to you, no matter what abuses might have been done unto you as a child, no matter how badly you think you behaved, that authentic core of your being is intact. It can never be destroyed. It can only be masked by ego.

Freedom and joy come from listening to these voices and *not believing them.*

It is only with the heart that one can see rightly, what is essential is invisible to the eye.
ANTOINE DE
SAINT-EXUPERY

But I Always Do It That Way!

As we contemplate making our lives over to reflect our new perspectives, we must challenge our habitual ways of being in the world. Many of the ways we relate to aging are nothing more than habits—ingrained ways of looking at the world. Habits are part of our lifelong conditioning, but they aren't necessarily a problem. Some habits are biologically programmed into our brains to help us function more efficiently. It would be a real drag if every morning we had to put our full attention on how to make coffee, brush our teeth or drive a car. Once we develop proficiency for doing things a certain way, or consistently think about things in a predictable manner, our brains imprint it on our synapses so we can repeat the thought, emotion or action without much effort. The more you do something, the deeper the imprint (which is why it gets harder to change as we get older). It's like taking the same path to the water's edge every time you visit a lake surrounded by tall grass. Soon the grass gets beaten down and you've created an easy, habitual path.

The problem with habits is that they often become the *only* path we can see and we shift into autopilot. Ever pull in to your destination and wonder how you got there?

Habitual patterns don't allow for direct experience or conscious choice. They fail in situations or opportunities that call for a new point of view or creative solution. When we come up against experiences where habits won't suffice, we are startled into conscious awareness. Having so often relied on habitual programming, we become anxious, not sure what to do. Then we come up with all sorts of rationalizations to help explain away these feelings and settle comfortably back into our habitual ways of being. We go back to sleep, missing the opportunity to create a different path to another part of the lake, or choose a different destination altogether.[74]

Try putting your keys in a different location for a week. Notice how you continually go back to the same place to get them, even when you *know* you have moved them. Frustrating, isn't it?

Habits drive our lives, beliefs, expectations, and the way we are in the world. While it may simplify our lives to leave our keys in the same place every time, how can we grow and adapt to a changing set of circumstances (i.e., growing older, rounder, grayer) if we continually rely on habitual ways of interacting with the world? It's tough. To change, we have to create new synaptic connections that support *consciously* chosen responses, beliefs and behaviors.

How do we challenge these habitual ways of interacting with the world? By consciously changing what or how we do everyday things: take a different route to the grocery store; move the trashcan to a new location; sit in a different chair at the dinner table; stand in a different spot in exercise class.

After all, no matter how many times you told yourself that the keys moved, you went back to the original location, right? Each time you do that, you're rewarded with a little wake-up call. *Oh, I remember, I put my keys over there!* Do it enough times and it becomes easier to remember to look in the new location. Congratulations! You have successfully created new synaptic connections in your brain.

If you take this example of behavioral habit (looking in the same place for your keys) and you extend it to look at habitual feelings (e.g., always thinking the same thoughts when you feel angry), or habitual reactions to change (*no!*), or habitual resistance to aging (*wrinkles*? No way, give me *Botox*!), you can see how programmed we really are. When we are identified with our egocentric conditioning (when we think the ego is *who we are*), we react automatically. Conditioning is our default setting, and we always revert to it unless we are consciously living in the moment.

Once we are aware of this process, we can begin to disconnect from the voices of conditioning and live joyfully in the present. It doesn't just happen—we have to practice!

Castrating an Ego

The only problem with not castrating
A gigantic ego is
That it will surely become amorous
And father
A hundred screaming ideas and kids
Who will then all quickly grow up
And skillfully proceed
To run up every imaginable debt
And complication of which your brain
Can conceive.
This would concern normal parents
And any seekers of freedom
And the local merchants nearby
  As well.
They could very easily become forced
To disturb your peace;
All those worries and bills could turn to
  Wailing ghosts.
The only problem with not lassoing
A runaway ego is
You won't have much desire to sing
  In this sweet
  World.

HAFIZ OF SHIRAZ

CHAPTER 20

Practice Makes Present

A S I ENTERED MY forties and fifties, I found it essential to reset my spiritual anchor. Simple practices—sitting still, mindful walking, yoga—reconnected me with that sense of oneness with all of life. Over the years, my spiritual practice has both grounded me and given me wings, offering true joy and the knowingness that I can live fully in every moment as it happens. The more I practice, the more I am able to be present. The more present I am, the more joyful life is, regardless of external circumstances.

Today is where life is happening. Every day is a fresh start. You can never step in the same stream twice. Every moment is new. So, how does one learn to live in the present moment? Well, if you want to play the guitar, you practice. If you want to excel at dance, you practice. If you want to spend more time in the present—practice!

There are so many ways to practice keeping your attention in the present, each with its own unique gifts. Explore your options. Find a practice that allows you to relax your body and focus your mind. You may be

And if there is not any such thing as a long time, nor the rest of your lives, nor from now on, but there is only now, why then now is the thing to praise and I am very happy with it.

ERNEST HEMINGWAY

Awake. Be the witness of your thoughts. You are what observes, not what you observe.

GAUTAMA BUDDHA

If we were not so single-minded about keeping our lives moving,
and for once could do nothing,
perhaps a huge silence might interrupt this sadness
of never understanding ourselves
and of threatening ourselves with death.

PABLO NERUDA

drawn to prayer, sitting meditation, moving meditation or yoga, conscious breathing, visualization or Tai Chi. Do whatever feels like a fit for you.

No matter what your age and which practice you choose, it's important to integrate your practice into your daily schedule. In fact, make it as important yet ordinary as brushing your teeth! Do you awaken each morning and argue with yourself about whether you're going to brush your teeth or not? Perhaps you did as a child, but then you learned about painful cavities and bad breath, and now you just do it without all the inner dialogue. The same applies to your awareness practice. Schedule it in and just do it.

Intrinsically, most of us know how important it is to integrate stillness, quiet, and a sense of peace into our everyday lives. We just don't choose it. Here's an opportunity to make a fresh start in living more mindfully. In the following pages, I'll give you a brief introduction into several practices. It doesn't matter where you begin, because after you practice any type of meditation for a while, you'll start to see your whole life as an opportunity to practice awareness.

There is a seeming paradox in mindfulness training. Most people think there is somewhere to get to, something to do. The best way to get "there" is to be "here." According to author Gertrude Stein, "There is no *there* there." While she was actually referring to a place she couldn't find, she also hit on a profound spiritual truth: there is no *there;* all we have is *here*. A mindfulness practice is a ticket to nowhere (else)—in other words, it's a ticket to *now*.

Meditation

Meditation is simply the practice of paying attention to each moment as it arises. There is no way to do it wrong. There is no "good" or "bad" meditation. There is simply paying attention.

Meditation trains the mind to be fully relaxed and alert. An ongoing meditation practice trains the mind much like exercise trains the body. Anyone can exercise; anyone can meditate. Honestly, I don't love to meditate. I just love how my life *works* when I meditate regularly. I'm not stressed, I can focus, I'm more creative, and it's easier to keep things in perspective. Life just flows.

Meditation brings forth a clarity that allows us to stop reacting and start responding, consciously, to whatever the moment holds. It's about noticing the constant chatter in your head that tries to run your life. Once you see it, you have the choice to ignore the chatter and be in the present moment.

Meditation is not a new-age phenomenon. It's a tool that has been used for centuries to facilitate awareness and spiritual awakening. Today, even large corporations offer meditation classes. Executives in the boardroom sometimes sit in quiet contemplation before a meeting. Meditation brings forth a clarity that allows one to break from reactive conditioning and respond more creatively to whatever the moment holds. It's a portal to the present.

According to *Yoga Journal*:

> *When the mind is able to focus on what is relevant to what is happening now, we experience ourselves as being one with what we perceive. This experience is deeply joyful, as we become freed from the illusion that we are separate from everything else in the universe. In fact, meditation isn't a withdrawal from life but a deeper, fuller presence in life.... It is this ability to be*

Walk slowly. Don't rush. Each step brings you to the best moment of your life; the present moment.
THICH NHAT HANH

Don't just do something—sit there!
SYLVIA BOORSTEIN

both extremely relaxed and alert that best describes the meditative state.[75]

The greatest weapon against stress is our ability to choose one thought over another.
WILLIAM JAMES

Meditation offers many health benefits to an aging body, and to the soul as well. In his groundbreaking book *The Relaxation Response*, Dr. Herbert Benson of Harvard Medical School presented a meditation technique to help people deal with stress. To this day, his methodology is recommended by health-care professionals as a way of lowering blood pressure and respiratory rate, slowing heart rate and ridding the body of stress hormones, which can cause heart disease and strokes. It also happens to be a wonderful mindfulness practice. Here is a quick overview of the technique:

- Sit comfortably, with eyes closed.
- Pay attention to your breathing, and repeat a word or phrase silently to yourself as you exhale.
- When you notice your mind wandering (*trust me, it will*), just notice it and gently bring your attention back to your breath, phrase or prayer.
- Practice for about 20 minutes each day, or at least three to four times per week.

There are many styles of meditation to choose from, both open- and closed-eye versions. Do some exploring and choose a style that works for you. There are many benefits.

Studies measuring the biological markers of aging (vision, hearing and blood pressure) found that meditators were physically younger than their chronological age.

Researchers have found that meditating lowers levels of stress hormones, and therefore supports the healthy functioning of the immune system. In fact, by decreasing the level of one such hormone—epinephrine—meditation has been shown to reduce the amount of cholesterol in the blood and therefore help arteries to remain clear. People who meditate also show improved blood circulation, which protects the arteries; lowered blood levels of lactic acid, which is associated with anxiety; and lowered heart rate, which places less demand on the heart.[76]

Meditation also synchronizes our brain and balances our right and left hemispheres. Most of us tend to use one side of our brain more than the other. When we have a lot on our plates, one side of the brain goes into overload, resulting in an overall sense of unease and anxiety. The next time your life feels out of balance, let go of the need to think or plan your way out of your situation. Instead, sit still and focus on your breath, a prayer or a mantra. By integrating the two sides of your brain, you create the space for innovative solutions to arise. It's why we often have our best ideas in the shower!

Many of us have an occasional meditation or prayer practice sandwiched into our busy lives. It's easy to let it fall by the wayside. Your inner voices will try their darndest to keep you from meditating. They will tell you it's too hard, you don't know how, you don't have the time, you have more important things to do, you don't like it, you're not doing it right and so on. Stick with it! Acknowledge the voices—and meditate anyway. Be consistent; make it part of your everyday routine. After all, you want to be present for *every* day of your life, don't you?

Sitting in meditation is like watching a bus go by filled with raucous partygoers… and girl, *it's noisy in there!* It's okay to watch the bus go by, we only get into trouble when we get onboard and join the party. Instead, just notice the bus going by and bring your awareness back to the breath.

Meditation is not a way to enlightenment nor is it a method of achieving anything at all. It is peace and blessedness itself.

DOGEN ZENJI

Consciousness gives you choices. After you have meditated for a while, you will notice that the spirit of mindfulness being cultivated while you are sitting still will spill over into your daily life. You will find your ability to pay attention to what are doing, whom you are with and the things around you increasing. While it may not be easy, it is *so* worth it. Ultimately, *om* is where the heart is.

There are many ways to cultivate awareness, including moving meditations. Here are some additional practices you might consider for an aging body with a timeless spirit.

Yoga is a series of specific poses that stretch and realign the body (among other things). It is gentle and non-competitive, and requires only that you pay attention and breathe into the postures, doing only what is comfortable for you. Your body will benefit from increased blood flow, flexibility and bone density, and your inner chatter will quiet down as well. I attribute my now healthy back to my yoga practice.

The yogic tradition focuses on the interconnectedness of everything. According to *Yoga Journal,*

> *…yoga (or union) happens when the mind becomes quiet. This mental stillness is created by bringing the body, mind, and senses into balance, which in turn, relaxes the nervous system. Meditation begins when we discover that our never-ending quest to possess things and our continual craving for pleasure and security can never be satisfied. When we finally realize this, our external quest turns inward, and we have shifted into the realm of meditation.*[77]

Every yoga tradition has a slightly different focus, so try a variety to find one that meets your needs. Be sure to ask about the instructor's credentials and experience— it's your body! *(Note: If you have any ongoing medical conditions, check with your doctor before starting any physical practice.)*

Tai Chi is a combination of yoga and meditation in movement, with roots in Chinese martial arts. It is a series of soft, graceful movements that bring about physical, emotional, spiritual and energetic balance. Its relaxing and meditative effect is one of the primary reasons people are drawn to the practice.

Tai Chi also offers many documented health benefits: lowering stress, regulating heart rate and breathing, and increasing muscle tone. It is practiced slowly, allowing one to develop a relaxed focus, which ultimately benefits the entire nervous system.

Qigong (pronounced chee gung) uses controlled breathing, movement, and meditation to manage one's life energy (chi). Visualizations are used to enhance the mind/body connection and support healing. According to the Qigong Association of America, regular qigong can prevent and treat illness, reduce stress, establish balance, integrate mind/body/spirit and bring peace.[78]

Walking meditation just might be the easiest practice to incorporate into your life. You can do it anywhere, anytime, and it's as simple as this: As you walk at a normal pace (preferably alone), focus your attention on the world around you in the present moment—the sensations, sights, sounds and smells. Make specific observations. *The puffy cloud formations look like marshmallows. The trees are turning red and gold. The sweet alyssum smells divine. The earth is warm. The air is cool on my skin.* No judgment, no analysis, no opinions, just what *is*. When you find yourself rehashing yesterday's conversation, or thinking about what you have to do tomorrow, gently bring your attention back to the present, simply observing the world around you. *The sun is warm. The roses are in full bloom. Don't they ever cut their lawn?* Oops. Back to

Blessed are the flexible, for they shall not be bent out of shape.
UNKNOWN

When I dance, I dance; when I sleep, I sleep; yes, and when I walk alone in a beautiful orchard, if my thoughts drift to far-off matters for some part of the time, for some other part I lead them back to the walk, the orchard, the sweetness of this solitude, to myself.
MONTAIGNE

the present. *The roses smell sweet. The grass is soft*, and on and on.

Eating meditation—yes, there really is an eating meditation!—can be a simple, easy gateway to the world of meditation, or a very tasty addition to your established practice. Mindful eating is a natural part of conscious living.

Have you ever been unable to recall what you ate for dinner last night? That's probably not a "senior moment"—that's a zombie moment. You were barely there. Stop feeding the hungry ghost over the kitchen sink, and the couch potato in front of the television, and the multi-tasking bumble bee… do not read, watch TV or listen to music… just sit. And be a human, with food.

Look at the food on your plate; notice the colors, textures and smells. Place a bite in your mouth and put your utensil down. Savor the taste. Is it hot or cold; sweet, sour or spicy? Chew slowly and swallow completely before you take another bite. Give thanks for the gifts of nature and human effort that brought this nourishment before you. Appreciate every morsel.

Mala beads or **Rosary beads**—where moving meditation meets prayer. Used in several traditions around the world, mala beads are a strand (sometimes bracelet) of identical beads, and each time you touch a bead, you are reminded to return to your center, say a mantra or prayer, and take a breath. Similarly, rosary beads may be used to center yourself and replace your inner chatter with prayer. This practice reduces stress and helps to put things in proper perspective.

Centering Prayer

Many believe there is a separation between meditation (spirituality) and prayer (religion), but in truth, they are slightly different variations of the same process and have the same aim: to connect with the Divine. Contemplative prayer is an example of how prayer and meditation can merge. For the first 16 centuries of Christianity, contemplative prayer was a central aspect of the religion. With the Reformation and the dominance of rationalism, direct mystical experiences of God were discredited, and the tradition was lost. That is, until 1974, when Father Thomas Keating of St. Joseph's Abbey and his Trappist brother Father William Meninger created Centering Prayer.[79] Now a worldwide phenomenon, popular with both Catholics and non-Catholics alike, it has roots in a 14th century guide to meditation titled *The Cloud of Unknowing* (as well as in the writings of contemplatives Saint John of the Cross and Saint Teresa of Avila). The process asks one to find a quiet place to sit with eyes closed and surrender one's mind to God. A single word is used repeatedly to bring the mind back to this surrendered state. Sound familiar? The similarities between centering prayer and meditation are many.

Prayer is not an old woman's idle amusement. Properly understood and applied, it is the most potent instrument of action.

MAHATMA GANDHI

Ask, and it shall be given to you; seek, and you will find; knock, and it will be opened to you.

JESUS OF NAZARETH

Gratitude

There's a prevailing belief that "enough" is just a little more than anyone ever gets. What a recipe for disappointment and non-stop suffering!

Can you entertain the idea that we all have exactly what we need to be happy, but that the conditioned ego wants to keep us from experiencing it? It does so with thoughts of lack and limitation.

Expressing gratitude is a simple yet powerful practice of mindfulness used to counter thoughts of scarcity (living in *scare-city*). It can lift your mood and allow you to see with new eyes in a very short amount of time.

In the Bible, the disciple Paul says, "In everything, give thanks."[80] I believe he meant for *everything*, not just for the things you want or that please you. This is not a denial of life's difficulties or a Pollyanna approach to living, but rather an appreciation for the higher wisdom at play in our lives.

Years ago, I read a story that offered a helpful perspective:

> *An old Chinese man's only horse ran away. His neighbors consoled him and told him how unfortunate he was. The old man shrugged his shoulders and said, "We shall see." Shortly thereafter, the horse returned with a stallion by its side and the neighbors told him how fortunate he was! The old man replied, "We shall see." Shortly thereafter, the man's son was riding the stallion and fell off and broke his leg. Again the neighbors consoled him, exclaiming how bad this turn of events was. The man simply replied, "We shall see." Shortly after the son broke his leg, an army of soldiers came through town and conscripted all able-bodied men to fight. The old man's son was not called into service because his leg was still on the mend. The neighbors once again claimed how good this was. The old man in his wisdom responded, "We shall see."*
>
> – UNKNOWN

We may think we know what is good and bad, right and wrong, and we spend a lot of time and energy trying to be and get the right and good, and protect ourselves from the bad and wrong. We expend a lot of energy on things we often have no control over. I once heard it said that control is really our conditioned ego's attempt to keep our life small enough to fit its picture of how our world needs to be in order to keep us safe.[81] *Yikes!*

Expressing gratitude for *all* that happens in our lives allows us to break from this dualism and see that everything is just as it's meant to be. It's only our belief about something that gives it power and/or meaning.

No one really knows how all the pieces fit together. What may look like good news now can turn out to be very painful later on, and what we see as a hardship now can become a gift. Haven't some of your most painful experiences been your greatest lessons? After all, with most life crises, there is a silver lining—we simply have to be willing to look for it. In doing so, we light the way to a fresh perspective.

The words *gratitude* and *grace* both stem from the Latin word *gratus*, which means thankful or agreeable. A mindset of gratitude opens us up to see the blessings that grace our lives and to experience a deeper appreciation for all that we have.

As my true, authentic self re-emerges, I am often overcome with gratitude. It was within me all the time, like a seed waiting for the right conditions to sprout. Grounding myself in my spiritual practice, engaging in activities that support my connection to my inner self and not believing the limiting voices of conditioning have created ideal conditions to foster a sense of inner peace.

One day, as I wrote in my gratitude journal, I built a list of reasons to be grateful for my short, silver hair. Much to my surprise, the list just kept growing!

- No more toxins on my scalp
- I never have to spend long hours and lots of money at the hairdressers
- Stiff breezes are no longer a threat of root exposure

There is always a lot to be thankful for, if you take the time to look. For example, I'm sitting here thinking how nice it is that wrinkles don't hurt.

UNKNOWN

- It's easy to style, quick to dry, and looks good even in damp weather
- I can exercise any time of day because it's quick and easy to shower and be ready for the next adventure
- I feel authentic, natural—even sexy!

Now those are things to be grateful for. Gratitude is the currency of spiritual commerce. Spend freely… you can't run out!

What a wonderful life I've had! I only wish I'd realized it sooner.

COLETTE

Find a way to integrate gratitude into your life.

~ Make a commitment to yourself to begin and end each day by acknowledging the many gifts you have been graced with. Write them down or simply savor them in your mind.

~ Begin by creating a list of at least seven reasons to be grateful for aging gracefully. My list included:

I'm not (as) concerned with meeting someone else's standards.

I am able to say no without guilt.

I am more creative and have more time to explore things that interest me.

I've given up much of the drama in my life; most of it was a lot of fuss about nothing too important.

I tend to be more calm, relaxed, grounded and centered.

I can ask for what I want and give to others more freely.

I have a broader perspective on life, and I choose where I want to put my time, energy and money.

I'm willing to take a risk; failure doesn't seem quite so daunting.

*I don't want to be like anyone else; I'm more interested in being the authentic **me**.*

Many of us resist change, yet every moment is new. I love to practice what the Buddhists call "beginner's mind": seeing the world moment to moment, with fresh eyes, no expectations, and no judgments. Living mindfully, I can move effortlessly into the future—moment by moment. *That* is authentic living.

The Universe does not want you perfect, it wants you to be perfectly you. Find your true Self and you become peace.
UNKNOWN

Making Life Last Longer

Why is all this mindfulness training so important? Besides making your life more joyful and fulfilling, it will actually seem longer! While none of us really knows the *quantity* of life we have been granted, I've learned we can impact the *quality* of our life by living it mindfully.

Life is very much like a pot of water put on the stove to boil. If we give the pot our full attention as the water heats up, we see small bubbles slowly start to form, then dance under the surface. We notice steam swirl close to the surface and rise randomly. After a while, the water erupts in a wild jumble of bubbles, heat and steam. There is so much to see, so many details to notice. When we pay attention to the moment-by-moment process of water coming to a boil, the experience seems to fill up the time, and we see things we've never noticed before.

Compare that experience with the last time you made pasta: turning on the stove under a pot of water, then making a quick phone call while folding a pile of laundry. Suddenly that pot of water is screaming for attention and we don't know where the time went. It happened so quickly!

In actuality, both pots of water took the same amount of time to come to boil. With the first one, we experienced the process; with the second, we weren't paying attention and we missed it. It's kind of like life, don't you think? Have you found yourself saying, "Where did the years go? Where was I when *that* happened? How did she/he get to be a teenager so quickly? I've lived here five years already?" These questions are indicators that you may not be as present to your life as you'd like.

As I moved through my fifties, I became keenly aware of the diminishing number of years I had left on this planet. When I wasted time on activities that brought little joy and satisfaction, I found myself asking: *How will I make the most of my time? How will I make a difference? How will I live my life with purpose?* Deepening my awareness was key to making choices that were in alignment with my authentic nature, my values and my intentions.

We hear it all the time—pay attention, live in the moment, be conscious, live mindfully—but what does it really mean? Mindfulness is the act of being engaged in and paying deliberate attention to one's life experience as it is occurring, without judgment. Why? Because life feels longer, fuller and richer when you're present with what is happening here and now, and you appreciate life as it unfolds, moment by moment.

When a noble life has prepared old age, it is not decline that it reveals, but the first days of immortality.
MURIEL SPARK

I've read about people who have had near-death experiences. They often speak of their renewed sense of how precious life is. They understand the gift they have been given and they don't want to waste a minute of it. They no longer fear death, which gives them a leg up on the rest of us!

As for the rest of us, many would rather be anywhere but right where we are. Have you ever seen those bumper stickers that say, "I'd rather be (shopping, on vacation, fishing, sleeping, etc.)"? *That's what I'm talking about!* That mindset costs us the joy of experiencing life as it happens—and puts us at risk of missing the whole adventure.

Consciousness gives you choices. Be here now. There really is nowhere else to be.

We never know when something that appears "bad" in the short term will turn out to be "good" in the long run. By letting go of the need to evaluate, we can be present to whatever arises in the moment.

Taking Care of Ourselves

One day, as my life was spinning out of control and I was erroneously taking it out on my husband, he turned to me and asked, "How long has it been since you've been on a retreat? You're always much nicer when you come home from one of those." (*ouch*) Wise man, and a good question.

It had been a looong time, nearly five years. Why had it been so long? Because I believed my inner voices when they told me I was too busy, too tired, couldn't afford it, didn't deserve it, or whatever creative excuse they could muster up. No wonder I was feeling adrift, out of sorts and hungry for something more. I had been looking to my external environment to give me what I needed. I had forgotten that rarely works. *Don't believe the voices!*

We can all benefit from taking time periodically to just *be* with ourselves. How else are we going to discover what we want to do when we grow up? Taking the time to slow down, quiet our minds and turn within is not only a good idea, it's necessary to help us uncover the latent dreams and desires that get buried in the noise of everyday life.

What excuses are your inner voices using to keep you from taking time for yourself? The thing to remember is that none of them are *true* until you choose to believe them.

It takes courage to grow up and turn out to be who you really are.
E.E. CUMMINGS

We can easily forgive a child who is afraid of the dark; the real tragedy of life is when adults are afraid of the light.
PLATO

Happy new day!

It seems a lot of us take better care of our cars than we do ourselves. Give yourself permission to go in for a tune-up!

I invite you to join me in my new annual tradition of attending a retreat sometime during your birthday month. There is something very sweet about celebrating one's birth in intimate company with one's self, honoring the woman you've become. Use this time to celebrate the beginning of your personal New Year and set clear intentions for how you want to live the coming year.

You might find that having your own New Year celebration makes it unnecessary to set January 1st goals. This new tradition is about setting *intentions*, not goals, and appreciating that each new day deserves to be celebrated.

I find that when I take good care of myself, I have more to give to those I love. I'm more patient, more understanding, and more loving once I recharge my own batteries. Feeling nurtured, I am more available to connect with those around me, and I am able to do so on a deeper level. To create more intimacy with others, I must first experience it within myself.

Some of you may be thinking, "I could *never* go away on a personal retreat. I have obligations, family, etc." Others may be thinking, "I would never *want* to do that!" Again, you have to find your own path, your own sanctuary. While it's best to change your venue and get away from the expectations of your everyday life, you don't have to go for long periods of time.

While we each need time to renew and recharge, we're all different in how to best meet that need. Tune in and see what you need to replenish your soul. If a retreat seems daunting, explore other ways to recharge, such as travel, prayer, yoga, meditation, a long run, time alone, or maybe a combination of these options. What is it for you? Once

Insight comes out of being kind to yourself, not out of saying that you're broken and you need to be fixed, changed, made over. If you're willing to stay with your neurosis—not act it out, not repress it, not fix it—then your own wisdom guide will come forth.

PEMA CHODRON

you have your answer, research your options and *make it happen!*

What's that? I can hear your inner voices screaming from here. Don't believe them. Remember, they are not on your side.

The Power of Grace

L OOKING BACK OVER MY life, I am grateful for the many moments of grace I've been gifted with. Each one pointed me towards new levels of insight and understanding, giving me the choice to let go of the old and embrace something new. This has been especially true during these midlife years.

I now appreciate that my salon epiphany was truly a gift of grace, an experience that snapped up the shades and let in the light. It was time for a change, time to face the monster hiding under the bed, time to look through a new lens and bring the bigger picture into focus. For many of us, letting go of our fears about aging, understanding the opportunities that lie ahead, reclaiming our slumbering dreams and redefining who we want to be for the rest of our lives is truly the most important work we have done to create a fresh start for ourselves. Congratulations on reclaiming your life!

As I bear witness to my journey, I see I was guided by some basic life principles, which I used as stepping-stones to traverse the turbulent waters of my conditioning:

                                   Gratitude
                                   Respect
                                   Awareness/Acceptance
                                   Compassion
                                   Equanimity

Embracing each of these principles helped me open up to and accept the inevitable passage of time and see my life as the gift it truly is. As the years pass I sometimes forget that *I am integral to all that is.* I slip back into the drama of everyday life and sleepwalk once again, continuing to see myself as separate. Thankfully, a part of me always knows the truth—a knowingness that is available to each of us.

We are all connected and adequate in every way possible. When I allow this to sink in, my rounding middle, sagging skin and deepening wrinkles seem so inconsequential. When I shine the soft light of compassion on my human fears and concerns, I can dip into that deep well of kindness and be reminded once again that *Everything Is All Right.* I often turn to the power of these principles to bring me back to now.

Kindness in words creates confidence. Kindness in thinking creates profoundness. Kindness in giving creates love.

LAO-TZU

Gratitude

Gratitude for getting older? For hot flashes? For going gray? For a rounder figure, sagging skin and wrinkles? *Yes!* To live fully, you must embrace it all.

Life is a process, with each stage bringing blessings and challenges. It's important to feel gratitude for *all* of it—not just for the good things in life, but also for the challenges and struggles. (*Especially* the challenges—no one ever gets stronger by coasting.)

Spend time each day appreciating the bounty of your life, as nothing brings you back to the present moment like filling your heart with thanks. Be grateful for the chance to turn gray; there are many who never made it this far. Thank your body for carrying you around for yet another day. Give thanks for the healthy food choices available to you, the beauty of nature and another lovely sunset. Be grateful for music and art and the way it opens your heart. Be deeply grateful for children and grandchildren to love and play with, and give thanks for the family and friends who love you—and who give you the opportunity to love in return.

Extend your gratitude to the people who make you want to tear out your hair in frustration, as they provide you with an opportunity to look within and see which parts of you need attention. Be grateful for the callous attitudes of others, as they remind you that no one can make you feel invisible or unimportant unless you let them. Be grateful for the experience of being offended, so you know what it feels like to others when you behave with indifference.

I found that the more gratitude I express for all that I have in my life, the more I have in my life to be grateful for!

As you lay your head to rest on your pillow each night, reflect on what you are grateful for. Rather than drift off with a head full of *I need to, I should, I hope I remember to…* take it down a notch and fill your heart with gratitude. It surely makes for better dreams.

A bit of the fragrance clings to the hand that gives the flowers.
CHINESE PROVERB

R-e-s-p-e-c-t

Find out what it means to me—Aretha was right! Respect is the foundation for a healthy sense of self. Without respect for ourselves (and others), we will give in to others' ideas of what we *should* be, do or have. There is a wonderful and oft-quoted line from Eleanor Roosevelt that reads, "No one can make you feel inferior without your consent." We teach others how to treat us, and that process starts with the level of respect we hold for ourselves. The quality of your relationships will improve greatly when you begin to truly love and respect yourself, hold your head up high, look the world in the eye, and know that there is nothing wrong with you. You are perfect just as you are, at whatever stage of life you happen to be.

In his book *The Six Pillars of Self-Esteem*, Nathaniel Brandon suggests that a healthy self-esteem is to the psyche what a healthy immune system is to the body.[82] When you have a healthy immune system, you may not be bulletproof, but when you do get sick or injured, you recover more quickly. The same is true with a healthy self-esteem. When life gets tough, you're less likely to be down for long. You have the inner strength to put things in perspective, stand up, brush yourself off and begin again.

As we age, it's important to respect the process of life and revel in the gifts of being an elder wise-woman. Would you really want to be 20 again and go through all that drama? No thank you!

Respect yourself enough to create the life you've always wanted—now. The next time you visit your hairstylist and they ask if you'd like something for the gray hair, say, "Yes—*respect!*"

Awareness and Acceptance

Awareness and acceptance are the cornerstones of a healthy and graceful aging process.

Be aware that your sense of reality is shaped by media exposure to countless images of what women are "supposed" to look like. Be aware that popular standards of worth are manufactured by the media and inherited from others. Be aware of your need to conform. Go within and define guidelines that are authentically yours.

Kindness is the mark of faith; and whoever has not kindness has not faith.

THE PROPHET
MOHAMMED

Examine the fears that drive you to alter yourself. Then, instead of giving in to them, accept that your body is changing, and keep it healthy and fit. Accept your intrinsic beauty and know that hanging on to the past only weighs us down, and will eventually sink us.

Nurture your dreams and live them fully. The present moment is all we truly have. Yesterday is just a thought, tomorrow a hope. When we stop doing everything else, peace and joy are what remain. Commit to a practice that will encourage you to live in the moment. Your happiness depends on it!

Compassion

We've all done things we're not proud of. We've made others wrong so we can be right. We've believed that "if you'll just be the person I want you to be, then I'll have a happy life." We've neglected, mutilated, dyed, chemically slathered and otherwise abused our physical bodies, trying to be the "right person" and forgetting we already are. We've abandoned our authentic selves in search of love and acceptance, forgetting it was within us all the time. We've lived most of our lives in pursuit of a standard that no one ever attains.

How can you *not* have compassion for one who has suffered so much?

Joy is compassion turned inward. First and foremost, nurture compassion for yourself and the suffering you have endured under the tyranny of your own mind. Compassion for yourself allows you to extend that compassion to others, and to give back to the world in ways that bring you joy and light you up from within. Out of this compassion, we can choose to live life moment to moment, knowing that this is all there is.

Compassion directed toward oneself is true humility.
SIMONE WEIL

Equanimity

Equanimity is a wonderful word that suggests balance, composure, calm and presence of mind.

For much of my life, I've had one foot in each of two different worlds. One was the world of girly glamour, where my looks were so important and maintaining the illusion of being the right person mattered—a lot. The other foot was in the spiritual realm, where outward appearance was irrelevant and what really mattered was being true to my soul and living a life in service to others. Paying attention to looking good felt like a betrayal of my spiritual self, but I wasn't willing to give up either pursuit.

I now understand there is only one authentic self, which allows me to keep both feet planted firmly beneath me. By continuing to live in the present moment, I can sense where to step next. There is only one world, the one to which I am present. Balance your life by honoring your body, mind and spirit.

Everything Is All Right

In the movie *Calendar Girls*, Miss February recalls her late nursery-owner husband saying, "The flowers of Yorkshire are like the women of Yorkshire; every stage of their growth has its own beauty, but the last stage is the most glorious." Indeed!

The crinkles around your eyes, the creases across your forehead, and the soft grooves from your nose to your mouth are all signs that you have loved, laughed, cried, frowned and *lived* the life you've been gifted.

It may have been grace that guided me on this journey, but I was not always graceful. Sometimes the lessons crept up on me gently, other times they were a smack upside my head. When I finally stopped long enough to pay attention, they always brought wonderfully transformative insights and kernels of wisdom that allowed me to see the world (and myself) like never before.

Now, I choose to embrace Mother Nature. I want to feel the soft wind blowing through my silver locks as I cruise into the rest of my life. I love the feel of the sun on my naked (okay, sun-screened) face. Nature… nurture… natural.

Everyone is the age of their heart.
GUATEMALAN PROVERB

My wish is that eventually we all stop second-guessing Mother Nature and learn to accept our true nature. When you nurture and accept all of your human experience through the compassionate lens of your spiritual nature, authentic beauty is as clear as day. Guided by the power of grace, we step into the gifts and opportunities that lie within, one precious moment at a time.

Looking back through the kaleidoscope of our lives, we bear witness to our journey. As Amazing Grays, we recognize that our blessings outweigh our aches and pains. We have learned to fully inhabit the body we have. We grieve our losses. We accept our role as wise-woman and acknowledge the sacred journey we are on. We leave the ghosts from the past and become a tenderhearted witness for our human side, which wants nothing more than to be loved, accepted and cared for. We know our ability to experience joy will be in direct proportion to how committed we are to living in the present moment.

By honoring and celebrating the aging process, we leave a legacy of authenticity for those who follow. We do it for ourselves, our daughters and granddaughters, and ultimately, for all women.

As T.S. Elliot so wisely put it, "And the end of all our exploring will be to arrive where we started and know the place for the first time." A *fresh* start.

For a list of books and resources, visit
www.maggiecrane.com

❦

The time will come when, with elation, you will greet
  yourself arriving at your own door, in your own mirror,
  and each will smile at the other's welcome.
And say...sit here. Eat.
You will love again the stranger who was your self.
Give wine. Give bread. Give back your heart to itself,
to the stranger who has loved you all your life, whom you
ignored for another, who knows you by heart.
Take down the love letters from the bookshelf, the
  photographs, the desperate notes.
Peel your own image from the mirror.
Sit. Feast on your life.

DEREK WALCOTT

Endnotes

1 Adler, Jerry. "The Boomer Files: Hitting 60." *Newsweek,* November 14, 2005.

2 Ibid.

3 Brooks, David. *Bobos in Paradise: The New Upper Class and How They Got There.* New York: Simon & Schuster, Touchstone, 2000.

4 Langer, Ellen. *Mindfulness.* Cambridge, MA: Perseus Books, 1989.

5 Jeffers, Susan. *Feel the Fear…and Do It Anyway.* New York: Ballantine Books, 1987.

6 Maslow, Abraham. *Toward a Psychology of Being,* 3rd Edition. New York: John Wiley & Sons, 1999.

7 www.raderprograms.com.

8 MSNBC study on aging: www.msnbc.com.

9 Huber, Cheri. *When You're Falling, Dive.* Murphys, CA: Keep It Simple Press, 2003.

10 Kubler-Ross, Elisabeth. On Death and Dying. New York: Macmillan Company, 1976.

11 Lara, Adair, "Who You Callin' Grandma?" *More,* November 2005.

12 Simon, Harvey. *The No Sweat Exercise Plan: Harvard Medical School Guides.* New York: McGraw Hill, 2006.

13 Lodge, Henry and Crowley, Chris. *Younger Next Year for Women.* New York: Workman Publishing Company, 2005.

14 Menec, Verena, "The Relation Between Everyday Activities and Successful Aging: A 6-Year Longitudinal Study." *Journal of Gerontology,* 2003.

[15] Bihova, Dr. Diana, clinical assistant professor of dermatology at New York University Medical Center.

[16] Patlak, Margie. "Hair Dye Dilemmas." *FDA Consumer,* April 1993.

[17] "Cosmetic Ingredient Review," 2005 CIR Compendium: www.cir-safety.org.

[18] Andrew, Angeline, et al. "Bladder cancer risk and personal hair dye use." *International Journal of Cancer* 109, no. 4 (April 2004) and Sanchez-Guerrero, Jorge, et al. "Hair dye use and the risk of developing systemic lupus erythematosus: A cohort study." Arthritis & Rheumatism, April 1996.

[19] University of Southern California, Keck School of Medicine, and International Journal of Cancer, February 2001.

[20] Cosmetic, Toiletry and Fragrance Association statement on Hair Dye, August 2006.

[21] Zheng, Tongzhang, ScD. Yale University researcher. American Journal of Epidemiology, January 15, 2004.

[22] The Nurses Health Study established in 1976, and the Nurses Health Study II established in 1989 by Dr. Walter Willett, in conjunction with Channing Laboratory and the surrounding medical community at Harvard Medical School.

[23] Takkouche, Bahi, MD, PhD; Etminan, Mallar, PharmD, MSc; and Montes-Martínez, Agustín, MD, PhD. "Personal Use of Hair Dyes and Risk of Cancer: A Meta-analysis." *JAMA* 293 (2005): 2516-25.

[24] *Chemical Research in Toxicology,* by the FDA's National Center for Toxicological Research, published September 2003.

[25] Erickson, Kim. *Drop-Dead Gorgeous.* New York: McGraw Hill, 2002.

[26] *Skin Deep,* a study conducted by the Environmental Working Group, published June 2004.

[27] Taylor, Shelley. *The Tending Instinct.* New York: Time Books, 2002.

[28] Christiane Northrup, M.D. *The Wisdom of Menopause.* New York: Bantam Books, 2001, 2006. Used by permission of Bantam Books, a division of Random House, Inc.

[29] Ibid.

[30] Ibid.

[31] Borysenko, Joan. *A Woman's Book of Life.* New York: Penguin Putnam, Riverhead Books, 1996.

[32] Ibid.

[33] Suzanne Somers. *The Sexy Years: Discover the Hormone Connection: The Secret To Fabulous Sex, Great Health, and Vitality, For Women and Men.* New York: Crown Publishers, 2004. Used by permission of Crown Publishers, a division of Random House, Inc.

[34] Ravdin, Peter, M.D. University of Texas, Anderson Cancer Center.

[35] *Los Angeles Times* article: "Breast Cancer Death Rate Bolsters Hormone Theory." Written by Thomas H. Maugh II. April 19, 2007.

[36] Wright, Jonathan, and Morgenthaler, John. *Natural Hormone Replacement for Women Over 45.* Petaluma, CA: Smart Publications, 1997.

[37] Ibid.

[38] Weed, Susan. *New Menopausal Years.* Woodstock, NY: Ash Tree Publishing, 2002.

[39] "metabolism." *The American Heritage® Science Dictionary.* Houghton Mifflin Company. 11 Jan. 2007.

[40] Schwarzbein, Diana, with Brown, Marilyn. *The Schwarzbein Principle II.* Deerfield Beach, FL: Health Communications, Inc., 2002.

[41] Ibid.

[42] Suzanne Somers. *The Sexy Years: Discover the Hormone Connection: The Secret To Fabulous Sex, Great Health, and Vitality, For Women and Men.* New York: Crown Publishers, 2004. Used by permission of Crown Publishers, a division of Random House, Inc.

[43] Schwarzbein, Diana, with Brown, Marilyn. *The Schwarzbein Principle II.* Deerfield Beach, FL: Health Communications, Inc., 2002.

[44] Weed, Susan. *New Menopausal Years: The Wise Woman Way, Alternative Approaches for Women 30–90.* Woodstock, NY: Ash Tree Publishing, 2002.

[45] Christiane Northrup, M.D. The Wisdom of Menopause. New York: Bantam Books, 2001, 2006. Used by permission of Bantam Books, a division of Random House, Inc.

[46] Huang, Z., et al. Harvard Medical School, Cambridge, MA. 1999.

[47] "Bare Bones: How to Keep Yours Strong." *Nutrition Action* Jan/Feb 2002.

[48] Fuchs, Nan Kathryn, PhD. "Calcium, Magnesium, and Aging." Women's Health Letter, July 2001. For more information visit www.womenshealthletter.com.

[49] Holick, Michael F. "Sunlight and vitamin D for bone health and prevention of autoimmune diseases, cancers, and cardiovascular disease." Presented at the conference "Vitamin D and Health in the 21st Century: Bone and Beyond," held in Bethesda, MD, October 9–10, 2003.

[50] "Memory Loss, Estrogen, Menopause and Alzheimer's Disease," Dr. Gayatri Devi, M.D., as reported at www.nymemory.org.

[51] Levy, Becca. "Mind Matters: Cognitive and Physical Effects of Aging Self-Stereotypes." Journal of Gerontology, July 2003.

[52] Langer, Ellen, PhD. Mindfulness. Reading, MA: Addison-Wesley, 1990.

[53] Marian Diamond, UC Berkeley, "Plasticity of the Aging Cerebral Cortex." Experimental Brain Research, 1982.

[54] Rosenweig, M., Bennett, E.L., and Diamond, M. "Brain Changes in Response to Experience." Scientific American 226, no. 2 (1972): 22-29.

[55] Joan Borysenko in an interview with Donna Strong in Awareness magazine, Jan/Feb 2005.

[56] "Sex After 40, 50 and Beyond." More, February 2005.

[57] Ibid.

[58] Ibid.

[59] eMedicinehealth.com.

[60] Northrup, Christiane, M.D. The Wisdom of Menopause. New York: Bantam Books, 2001, 2006, Bantam Books, a division of Random House, Inc.

[61] For more information, go to info@rainn.org.

[62] Heim, Dr. C., et al. "Pituitary-adrenal and autonomic responses to stress in women after sexual and physical abuse in childhood." JAMA 284 (5): 592-96.

[63] Hendrix, Harville, PhD. Getting the Love You Want. New York: Henry Holt, 1988; Owl Books, 2001.

[64] Beck, Martha. "The Halo Effect." O: The Oprah Magazine, December 2003.

[65] Christiane Northrup, M.D., *The Wisdom of Menopause*. New York: Bantam Books, 2001, 2006. Used by permission of Bantam Books, a division of Random House, Inc.

[66] Ibid.

[67] Spoken by Cheri Huber, American Zen teacher. www.livingcompassion.org.

[68] Stark, Lisa, and Carpenter, Megan. "Baby Boomers Challenge Notion of Retirement." ABC.go.com, January 10, 2006.

[69] Flora, Carlin. "Happy Hour." *Psychology Today,* Jan/Feb 2005.

[70] Stark, John. "Positive Outlook," *Yoga Journal,* Jan/Feb 2002.

[71] Adler, Jerry. "In Search of the Spiritual." *Newsweek,* Aug/Sep 2005.

[72] Fields, Rick. *Chop Wood Carry Water.* New York: Tarcher Publishing, 1984.

[73] Huber, Cheri. *When You're Falling, Dive.* Murphys, CA: Keep It Simple Books, 2003.

[74] Sikora, Mario. "The Notes and The Melody: Part IV." *The Enneagram Monthly,* July/Aug 2006.

[75] "Meditation for Everybody." *Yoga Journal,* Winter 2004 (special issue on Balanced Living).

[76] www.wholehealthmd.com.

[77] Carrico, Mara. "Yoga Basics," *Yoga Journal* online: www.yogajournal.com.

[78] Qigong Association of America, www.qi.org.

[79] Keating, Father Thomas. *Open Mind, Open Heart,* 20th Anniversary Edition. New York: Continuum International Publishing Group, 2006.

[80] *The Holy Bible,* Paul (1 Thessalonians, 5:18).

[81] Spoken by Cheri Huber, American Zen teacher, www.livingcompassion.org.

[82] Brandon, Nathaniel. *The Six Pillars of Self-Esteem.* New York: Bantam Books, 1995.